Mervyn Peake

a Personal Memoir

Mervyn Peake

a Personal Memoir
by
Gordon Smith

LONDON
VICTOR GOLLANCZ LTD
1984

First published in Great Britain 1984
by Victor Gollancz Ltd,
14 Henrietta Street, London WC2E 8QJ

Chapter One 'Hark! Ah, the Nightingale . . .' is a revised version
of a piece published in *The Mervyn Peake Review*,
issue 4 (Spring 1977)

British Library Cataloguing in Publication Data
Smith, Gordon, 1907—
  Mervyn Peake.
  1. Peake, Mervyn—Biography
  2. Novelists, English—20th century—
  Biography
  I. Title
  823'.912   PR6031.E183Z/

ISBN 0-575-03431-9

Designed by Leslie and Lorraine Gerry
Printed in Great Britain by
BAS Printers Limited, Over Wallop, Hampshire

To Maeve,
in affectionate memory

Contents

List of Illustrations

List of Photographs

Mervyn Peake and this Book

MERVYN PEAKE (1911–1968) has an established reputation as an artist. He was a draughtsman of genius, and has been called 'the best illustrator of our time'. He is also widely known as the author of *Titus Groan* and the other books of the 'Gormenghast' trilogy. It is slowly being realized that he was also an important and original poet—especially with the re-publication in *Peake's Progress* of 'The Rhyme of the Flying Bomb' and 'A Reverie of Bone'. But though he has become something of a cult-figure (especially among the young, in the universities, and in the United States of America), the power and human sympathy of his imagination have not been fully recognized by those who knew him only as a creator of bizarre drawings and fantastical worlds.

This book is not a critical study of his work. It is a personal memoir of a long and close friendship; and an attempt to give a picture—through his letters and through remembered incidents—of Mervyn Peake as he was. It may be argued that it does not matter what an artist or a writer was like, as a person. We can enjoy Shakespeare's plays even if we are crazy enough to believe that he was Bacon. The paintings of Monet and the poems of Baudelaire will demand an exact and relevant response from us whether we are familiar or not with the biographies. But just as some acquaintance with the historical and social background of a writer, and with the artistic aims and trends of his time, may make it easier for us to give the response, so some acquaintance with a writer's personality—whether he be Lamb or Oscar Wilde—will quicken our interest in his work. It may even help us to correct some preconceptions.

Mervyn has been fortunate in his commemorators so far, especially in two of them. John Watney's biography is sympathetic and accurate and has been authenticated by his close co-operation with Mervyn's wife Maeve and with many of his friends. In general assessments it is remarkable how often he has 'got it right'. I owe him a considerable debt, in checking his facts against my memory; and if I sometimes cover the same ground it is because I was there or, in many cases, even supplied the material.

The other writer is, of course, Maeve herself. Her book, *A World Away*, completed shortly before Mervyn's death, is a moving account of a long-sustained tragedy. It deals especially with his years of illness and frustration, and must paint therefore—as she admits—a slightly one-sided picture. The high spirits, the happiness and the hopes, so characteristic of his life generally, are told, but overlaid.

The present volume deals by contrast mainly with his younger days. I have written of his troubles during the War, as they are described in his many letters; and of later achievements; but his last years I have touched on far more briefly. We were close friends throughout his life. On the fly-leaf of her book, Maeve wrote: 'To Gordon—as Mervyn's only and best friend—with love from Maeve'; and in return I dedicate this volume to her memory.

The arrangement is generally chronological, though I have sometimes included future events to give a chapter unity; and I have prefaced my account of his life with a preliminary glimpse, a perhaps too flippant account of a trip we took together to the Auvergne in about 1930, when we were very young.

There are some difficulties in writing about a close friend. When Browning asked the man, 'And did you once see Shelley plain?', the answer seems to have been unsatisfactory. I never had any doubt that Mervyn was a genius, but—before that, and all the time—he was a person. I have tried to picture him as he looked and behaved; remembered the things we did together; recounted what he told me; and (more valuably) quoted from a number of his letters.

If, on any occasion, my approach has been less than reverential, it is not from any lack of affection or appreciation: and I do not think that Maeve would really have minded, since it was she above all who could reduce a situation to its proper absurdity with a mere twitch of her elegant nose. . . .

Hark! Ah, the Nightingale . . .

TERM WAS OVER, and as usual I hurried up to London to meet Mervyn. Our particular business was to arrange a short holiday in France. Those were the days when for ten pounds you could enjoy a fortnight's stay anywhere in Europe, including return fares, hotels, meals and pocket money. (But Scandinavia would cost you twelve pounds.) Mervyn had written about the projected trip, but we had not made any decision about where to go, except that it was to be France.

When he arrived at Piccadilly Circus he greeted me with his usual affectionate rudery. In a Bohemian way, he made quite a distinguished figure, rather like an artist out of *Trilby*; but I pointed out that he had six inches of scarlet pyjama trailing out at the bottoms of his corduroy trousers. Obviously he had got up in a hurry.

'Damn!' he said. 'And I was all dressed up for the great occasion. I *thought* people were staring at me rather more than usual.' He sounded quite upset, rather like Bertie Wooster when he found he was wearing only one spat; so to comfort him I took him into Lyons' Corner House, where we ordered coffee and poached eggs on toast. When he had finished, I produced a small map of France, torn from a travel agent's brochure. We eyed it thoughtfully.

'I tell you what,' said Mervyn. 'We'll shut our eyes, or rather, one of us will, and stick in a pin, and where it lands shall be our centre.'

I agreed, and he found a pin in his lapel and duly carried out the suggested operation. Not surprisingly perhaps, since the town was almost exactly in the middle of our map, the pin landed on Clermont-Ferrand. We knew nothing about Clermont-Ferrand, but we went down the street to Messrs Dean & Dawson's, where they sold us our return tickets. They seemed surprised that anyone should want to go to Clermont-Ferrand, but mentioned that there was a famous peak nearby called the Puy de Dôme.

'Stupendous!' said Mervyn, as we left. 'We will sit on top of the Puy de Dôme, and you shall write poems while I paint it.'

A few days later we set out. Nothing of particular note occurred on our journey as far as Paris, except that we saw Lord Baden-Powell sitting in the corner-seat of a railway carriage near Newhaven. This was fairly characteristic. If you bumped into anyone when out with Mervyn, it was as likely as not to be Mr. Churchill, and if you came across an animal it was often an elephant. (It will be seen later that I have not chosen these examples at random.)

In Paris we found a small hotel near the Madeleine, and set out at once to see the world. All I ever want to do in Paris is to wander about, and look at things, and perhaps have a meal or a drink. Mervyn shared my simple tastes, and we walked up the Champs Elysées discussing, rather childishly, the selection of an ideal World First Fifteen of painters. After considerable argument we agreed on a list of fourteen that included Rembrandt, Velasquez, Piero della Francesca and Botticelli. Leonardo, I think, was hooker. But we quarrelled about the last member of the side.

'For the last man,' said Mervyn firmly, 'we must have a stylist. I vote for le Nain. He can play wing three-quarter.'

'Le Nain!' I exclaimed in horror. 'Goats and monkeys! Don't be daft, he wouldn't even make the Extra C.'

But Mervyn shook his head obstinately, and we went back down to the Louvre to check. The attendant at the entrance remonstrated when he saw Mervyn about to go in with a pipe in his mouth; but Mervyn waved it at him to show that it was empty, and being a sensible Frenchman he made no further objection, not even suggesting that he should put it away in a pocket.

We gazed at the Victory of Samothrace and the Venus de Milo (so much more impressive than any of its replicas!), and argued again over the Mona Lisa. He said it was marvellous, and I said it still did nothing for me. On our way out we discovered a magnificent annexe full of Impressionists, and altered our side, quite monstrously, to include both Monet and Manet.

The State Railways of France finally deposited us at Clermont-Ferrand. It appeared to be a sort of French Wigan. Our bedroom had only one window, and that was jammed tight shut. When we had wrenched it, and the shutters, open, we found ourselves looking down on an enclosed public lavatory which smelt strongly of ammonia. So we shut everything hastily again, and went out into the street.

'One night here,' said Mervyn, waving his arms outside a fish-monger's shop, 'one night here will be a Plethora!' (He was fond of the word.) Just then his rucksack (which he was still carrying for some reason) burst. Indeed, it exploded. It was a mean little rucksack, tightly packed, and things went everywhere. . . . Three socks and a pair of travelling slippers landed among the soles and turbot, and his pyjamas were nearly carried away by a passing dog. We returned to our hotel in disgust.

The next morning, with the rucksack repaired (by me), we set off for the Puy de Dôme, which turned out to be a most charming hummock, like a miniature Fujiyama, set above the surrounding highlands. Clermont was much smaller in those days, and we were soon in open country. For some miles we played 'road-golf', which consists in driving a tennis-ball along the way with the handle of an ash-plant, taking alternate shots. It made us rather cross, as we kept finding the rough; so when we came upon an attractive inn still some miles before reaching the Puy, we decided to stay there. Indeed, we never did get round to climbing the Puy. Mervyn did some pleasant water-colours of the mountain (which I still possess), and flirted with the daughter of the patronne; while I wrote some fairly bad poems and tried, unsuccessfully, to persuade him of the philosophic virtues of Wordsworth.

Finally, after some days, we returned to Clermont and began

*1. From a School Autograph
Album (c. 1924)*

a leisurely return northwards, using our return tickets when we were too lazy to walk. Somewhere or other (I can't remember where now), there was a sharp wrangle about a greenish suit that caught Mervyn's eye. It was hanging among the outer ramifications of a little general shop in a village. The jacket was of a Norfolk tendency and the cut of the trousers oddly rakish. Mervyn fell for it at once. I objected, in my stolid English way, that he couldn't possibly wear a thing like that, even on holiday; that it wasn't likely to fit; and that he would be cheated over the price. However, when he tried it on, it fitted perfectly; the price was ridiculously low, and he wore it for the rest of the trip.

One night, we stayed in a really comfortable hotel, in a tiny village somewhere on the upper Allier. But after an excellent dinner we discovered that we had only just enough French money left to pay our bill, and that only if we did without breakfast. We had, it is true, one of those beautiful big white five-pound notes, enough to provide a week's comforts: but when we showed it to the patron he declared that he could not accept foreign currency, and that he had never seen anything like it in his life. We went to bed thoughtfully.

The next morning was bright and sunny. I got up, but Mervyn stayed in bed. 'There's nothing we can do until we get some more money,' he explained, 'and your French is better than mine. Go out and find a bank!' It was true that my French was better than his. From his unregenerate and even younger days he had picked up one or two phrases like 'Je m'en fiche!' and 'Baise-moi, Dulcie!', but they were of limited application and useless in a bank. So, having cursed him for his idleness, I set off.

Some women were beating their linen on the stones of the river, and they gave me directions. There was a bank, but it was three miles away, all uphill. When I reached it, finally, it was to see a notice which said 'Ouverte tous les autres jeudis'. But this was a Tuesday. The locals directed me further, to another village, and another bank. Another three miles away, and (this is all perfectly true) also uphill. This time the bank was open, and friendly, but they wouldn't change my five-pound note. They had never seen anything like it.

Downhill or not, it was a long way back to our hotel. Mervyn was still in bed.

I paid the bill with the remains of our French money. We had exactly three centimes left, and our return tickets on the railway. The station was only just across the valley, but there wasn't a train till four o'clock: so we sat among the pebbles of the almost dried-up riverbed, gloomily throwing small stones at each other's shins.

Finally, the train arrived, and we got in and trundled north to the splendid old town of La Charité. France being France, there was a Crédit Lyonnais still open; so we changed our money and made up for the long day's fast with an enormous meal.

It was the next day (I think), when we were wandering about the bushes and summer sand-flats of what had now become the Loire, that we decided to sleep out. This was partly a penance for our recent financial mismanagements, and partly because it seemed attractive. According to our map there was a hamlet hidden away somewhere, only a couple of miles off; so I left Mervyn happily painting by the water and set out to find it and buy some provisions.

The village was there all right, but it seemed to be uninhabited except by a large pack of hostile and vociferous dogs. I was becoming a little alarmed, when an upper window opened and an aged crone peered out. When she understood the situation she cursed the dogs shrilly and to such good effect that they all slunk away. After a little exploring I managed to purchase a long loaf, a bottle of wine and a tin of pâté, and went back to find Mervyn.

It was getting late, and the *maquis* sprawled everywhere. For a time I couldn't even find the river! By using the last pink glow in the sky I did at last find the spot where I had left Mervyn painting: but there was no sign of him. I searched all round, whistling 'Cherry Ripe!' as loudly as I could, and after twenty minutes elicited a faint and mournful reply. It was Mervyn. He was sad and alone. He had buried the two rucksacks in a sandbank for safety when he set off to meet me. It took us half an hour to find them.

By now it was nearly dark, but there was a moon coming up. We climbed a grassy hill that rounded up steeply from the river, and chose a spot where a single tree stood. It had become very cold. We put on all the clothes we had—pyjamas, sweaters and mackintoshes—over the top of our ordinary gear. We took off our shoes, put on extra socks, and laced our feet into the almost-emptied rucksacks, which we placed against the bole of the tree to prevent our rolling down the slope. But the tree, though sturdy, was not wide enough to stay both rucksacks, and one or the other of us kept losing his mooring. This led to a certain amount of bickering; but on the whole we decided that it was all worth it, in spite of the cold: for the scene was incredibly beautiful. The big river lay white in a curve below us, and the stars were huge. We set ourselves to sleep.

It was then that the nightingale arrived. . . .

He sat in the boughs, about ten feet above us, and sang. It was all Keats, and Matthew Arnold too. The long clear notes, getting faster, and the ecstatic bubble at the end: all held us entranced. After a time, his mate arrived, perched nearby, and answered him.

And they sang, and sang. But it was very cold, and we wanted to sleep.

'Bloody nightingales!' muttered Mervyn.

'Blasphemy!' I said, but I was beginning, guiltily, to agree.

The beautiful birds sang on. By two o'clock, I regret to confess, we were shouting at them, and even fell so low as to throw our shoes at them. We missed, of course, and the shoes rolled down the hill, and we had to retrieve them by a kind of sack-race hopping, like a couple of Sciapods.

At about four o'clock we finally gave up. We re-dressed, stumbled down to the flats, and set out to find the village. By five we had found it, and were greeted noisily by all the dogs. In England, at that hour, we would have been shut out, cursed, ignored, or told to wait. But here, in France, the bread was already baked, and soon there was steaming hot coffee too.

The rest of our journey back was comparatively uneventful, but it was all good. We were young, and in bounding spirits; and we returned to an equally exciting London, which was all ours for the taking. . . .

2. *Nude Study* (c. 1930)

A Small Public School

MERVYN AND I were at school together, but we might just possibly have met, long before that even, on the other side of the world.

My father was a dissenting minister (as Hazlitt would have put it) in the small walled city of Sinchow in Shansi, which is a remote hill-province in northern China. There, he preached to the killers of his immediate predecessors, set up schools, mapped the locations of tiny wolf-threatened out-stations, visited Buddhist monasteries and took rubbings of old Nestorian tablets. He organized relief work during the Great White Plague, built a church, and from time to time baptized a group of Christian converts in the small, tiled swimming-bath that was normally hidden under the pulpit.

When, in 1911, the Empress Dowager was overthrown and the Republic set up, not without some violence in the streets, my family fled to the coast at Tientsin, where we stayed in the German Concession. Goose-stepping Prussians in pickelhauben, French infantrymen and Zouaves, and the Somerset Light Infantry in scarlet with white pith helmets, all marched below our windows; and the steamers hooted on the Bund. . . .

Here, had I but known it, I was a close neighbour of the infant Mervyn, who was born that year. His father, a medical missionary, had come out even before the Boxer Rising, and had served through many dangers and adversities. Dr. Ernest Cromwell Peake (the names are characteristic of his time and profession) was a man of parts, solidly reliable, civilized and well-read, com-

Mervyn (right) with his brother, c. 1918

bining a gusty, jolly humour with gentleness—characteristics which he handed on to both his sons. Mrs. Peake was a little, brown-complexioned lady of great charm and strong character. I came to know her very well in later years, and we corresponded regularly from about 1930 onwards.

I remember Mervyn telling me how, as a child, he once stole away to his father's surgery, peering through the unguarded window to watch the amputation of a leg. 'I didn't mind,' he confessed, ''till the thing was off, when they put it on a tray and dumped it by the window, right underneath me. Then I keeled over.'

But I knew nothing of his childhood at the time. Our paths diverged again. We went back inland, to Shansi; and the Peakes remained east of us, or farther south. Mervyn went up to the mountain resort of Kuling, which he always recalled with pleasure because of its beauty, and later attended Tientsin Grammar School for a time, as a day-boy. My family, too, spent holidays in the mountains, in temples where the fifteen-foot-high idols glared down with contorted faces, and the strange slopes fell, mist-layered, like an old Sung painting.

Critics have speculated upon the extent and nature of China's influence upon Mervyn. In spite of his understandable interest in all things Chinese, such works as his distinguished series of drawings called *Quest for Sita*, and his long friendships with Sinophiles, from Laura Beckingsale and Eric Drake to Maurice Collis, this seems to me to be an unrewarding pursuit. Such cultural influence is difficult to pin down. But, like myself, Mervyn did speak Chinese as one of his two 'first languages', and knew the common people and the household servants on terms of intimacy. The children of the upper and middle classes, both in England and abroad, have always been saved from isolation and social blindness—at least till recently—by close contact with nannies and ayahs, house-boys and cow-boys, and the holders of stalls in the markets. The 'native-born', as Kipling calls them, inherit two home-countries.

Mervyn may have been influenced in his own manners by the good nature and simple humanity of the charming Chinese

Mervyn with his father, Tientsin, c. 1920

people: but their concept of 'the golden mean' is not an obvious characteristic of his own imagination and outlook.

Unlike him, I did not go to school, for there was none within range: so my mother taught me English, History, Geography and Arithmetic, while my father instructed me in the rudiments of Latin. But missionaries, having in many cases had to raise themselves to a decent level of education by their own efforts, were all determined that their sons and daughters should, at whatever personal sacrifice, receive good schooling. Leslie, Mervyn's elder brother, had been for a time a boarder at Chefoo School, an establishment of somewhat daunting piety on the coast, from which he emerged without scathe. Mervyn, as I have said, was briefly at Tientsin G.S. When my father went to France during the First War, I spent a couple of terms, one at a little school on Lake Erie, and one at Woodstock College, in Canada. But these were temporary measures. There were also public schools in England specially endowed to provide classes for missionaries' children, like Taunton School in Somerset, and Eltham College in Kent. It was to the latter that my brother and I, and Leslie and Mervyn Peake, were sent.

Eltham College ('School for the Sons of Missionaries', or 'S.S.M.') was situated near the village of Mottingham, eight miles or so out from Charing Cross. In those days there was open country all around. When, as a senior, I was one of the 'Hares' in the annual paper-chase (more strictly, it was a maize-chase, and very heavy the stuff was too!), I ran eleven miles through fields and woods and lanes and hardly saw a soul. Now, even the little River Quaggy runs under concrete.

The buildings had been erected to house the Naval College which later moved to Osborne. As you went up The Drive you had on your right first The Spinney, a wilderness full of known birds' nests, and then the Chapel, where there was a plaque to Prince Louis of Battenburg. There, when I was a prefect, I subjected the school to long declamations about Nebuchadnezzar and his image of gold, sparing them nothing of the 'harps, sackbuts, psalteries and all kinds of music'. There, according to my brother, though it was never proved, Mervyn set a chamber-pot in an inaccessible niche above the stalls. (Certainly, both he and my brother were beaten for cutting Sunday Evening Service.) There, too, dedicated Old Boys preached powerful and sentimental sermons: a professional hazard in such foundations, though we seem to have lived through it all without coming to much harm.

The main buildings, set about what then seemed to me an enormous quadrangle with cloisters on two sides, presented a respectable Georgian-style front; and there was a square Tower (all these places carried capital letters for us!), and a Swimming Bath, and a Sanatorium. The panelled Library (through which I ate my way like a locust, beginning with G. A. Henty, and ending with Horace), had a carved coat of arms with the motto 'Esto Perpetua'—another reminder of the Naval College, for our own motto was 'Gloria Filiorum Patres'.

The posts on the Front Pitch reminded visitors that this was a famous rugger school, and other playing fields extended beyond the tall trees of The Grove. Eric Liddell, the Olympic sprinter, scored innumerable tries (he was later to play for Scotland, with other Old Boys) on the 1st XV Pitch, by the Pond; and W. G. Grace had shown his doubts to an umpire on the Cricket square a few years before. There was a general feeling of space.

But when I arrived there, tense and lonely, the school cannot have been at its best. The long years of the First World War had depleted the Staff and lowered academic standards. There was no resident House Master at all; the food was poor; and far too much depended upon the authority of the prefects. The latter were effective, but I have seen black bruising from rump to thigh on one defiant offender after a prefects' beating. The place was neither vicious nor decadent, but those who were there then experienced something of Vigny's 'servitudes et grandeurs militaires'.

Just before Mervyn came to Eltham, however, there were important changes for the better. New masters arrived, notably Horace Pearson, who became House Master, and Eric and Burgess Drake, who transformed the English teaching. All three were to have a considerable influence on the young Mervyn Peake, and on me, as I shall try to show.

Mervyn arrived in 1923, a slim, dark youngster, to share a

double desk with my brother Harold, who became his close friend. Neither was an academic star, though both showed a flair for English, and Mervyn was soon much in demand by owners of autograph-albums when it was discovered that he could draw.

Leslie Peake was senior to me, but only by a year or two. Younger brothers in a public school being what they are, Leslie and I did not mix much socially with our 'minors', except perhaps to hand over a letter from home and keep a distant eye on their well-being. If my brother got into a fight (as he sometimes did, for he lacked my sense of caution), I would disperse the howling junior spectators and disentangle the two principals; if 'Pirate Peake' (as he soon became) had been 'lippy' to a senior and was in full flight, the appearance of his large walrus of a brother in the offing was enough to discourage the pursuer.

But, for a better understanding of the life we all led, perhaps I should say more about the new masters I have mentioned and the regime that they introduced. Horace Pearson (universally known as 'H.P.') was a kind but formidable figure: six foot three, with a beaked nose and hard arthritic hands. He was a powerful organizer. Paint reappeared upon the walls, the food improved, discipline was tightened, and the power of the prefects reduced — though they were still important and were allowed to cane. In the evenings, groups in dressing-gowns gathered in H.P.'s study in front of an open fire, with mugs of cocoa, to listen to gramophone records of classical music or hear talks by visitors on various topics.

H.P. was very good with the average boy, but his nonconformist outlook did not always comprehend the nonconformer. Art meant less to him than current affairs, and tended to mean a lantern-lecture on G. F. Watts. For Mervyn, therefore, he was not always a sympathetic character. There was a 'Black List' of those who had not been pulling their weight at work, and members of it were publicly rebuked at lunch on Thursdays. Mervyn was several times on this list. He would tell my brother, 'I really must do better this term, if only for my mother's sake.' But he soon slipped from grace. He was also pilloried for having 'forearms absolutely caked with dirt'; and this naturally hurt.

3. *The Dart Player*

Generally, he enjoyed school life; but he was sensitive, and resented sarcasm, unfairness or meaningless routine—as he did later in the Army. He was not 'against the system', for he was never a political animal, but he hated regimentation.

Much more congenial and important to him was the coming of the Drakes, Eric and H.B. These two brothers had been model pupils at the School, but had suffered, and read Freud, in the trenches; had taken first-class degrees in English; and now burst upon their old haunts with a mass of new ideas and unbounded enthusiasm. Both were brilliant teachers, and Eric was especially popular: an intellectual shower-bath, a rucksack-carrier, a fly-half who swore like a trooper when damaged, and (something of an awesome phenomenon to most of us) a professed atheist. (He too came from North China: indeed I could just remember staying with his parents; and his cousin, 'Ballar' Sowerby, who was a famous big-game hunter, once left a dead stag in our hall.)

So, experimental methods bloomed: 'Projects' and individual 'Assignments', personal anthologies and creative writing; and much splendid literature, classical and modern, was presented and devoured. Eric taught Mervyn and my brother Harold, and had considerable influence on them. Later, he was to set up an artists' colony in Sark, which led to Mervyn's long involvement with that remote and private island.

Some other members of the Staff influenced him, or caught his imagination for future use. There was McIver, the Art Master, who let him have his head; and Dr. Bakker, the huge, roaring French Master from Leyden, with white hair parted in the middle, who castigated all ill-doers as 'yotten plums' ('If there are ninety-nine good plums and one yotten plum, do the ninety-nine good plums make the one yotten plum good? No! The one yotten plum makes the ninety-nine good plums yotten too. And you, sir, are a yotten plum!'). He was a formidable figure, and appreciated as such by Mervyn, who hated several smaller, less direct, but more sarcastic teachers.

The Masters' Common Room, a shabby and inadequate place down the passage from the Central Hall, reappears in one of the Gormenghast books, as he used to glimpse it, skating past the half-open door: the petty squabbles, the anthracite fire, and the rows of shiny greenish gowns hanging from the wall. . . .

The Headmaster of the School was George Robertson, or 'Rabbi', who later went on to command George Watson's in Edinburgh. He was a Craven Scholar of Balliol, a double First in Classics and Maths; and though I doubt whether he was a great organizer, there are subtle advantages in having a really first-class mind around. Who shall say where the pollen may not have fallen? He caned, rather unusually, on the hand, with a rubber tube. Everybody knew that he showed a white neck when he played tennis, because of the high stiff collar that he normally wore; but he invented jet engines rather before their time and harnessed them to model boats which he made career across the Swimming Bath.

About this time, perhaps when I was in the Remove or the Fifth Form, I underwent an odd metamorphosis. Partly no doubt in self-defence, and partly because of a wayward sense of humour, I acquired a reputation for amiable daftness, and was given the unlovely name of 'Goat', or 'Goatie'—by which title, indeed, Mervyn addressed me or wrote to me throughout his life. After his death, Maeve reverted to 'Gordon', because my family called me that, and also because no woman cares much for the coarse nicknames men give each other.

There was very little real bullying at Eltham, though there were cliques and pecking-orders, and, inevitably, much thoughtless unkindness among the juniors. Nor was there much dishonesty or wild indiscipline. Nor was perversion rampant, though our only contact with the fair sex ('the hags') during term-time was on visits to or from our sister-establishment, Walthamstow Hall, at Sevenoaks. (The most unlikely boys turned out to have beautiful sisters at 'Snooks'!) On the whole we were curiously unsophisticated and—once we had each settled in—happy. 'Youth, thank Heaven,' as Kipling remarks of a not entirely dissimilar school, 'is its own prophylactic!'

We had no professional aesthetes. Mervyn and his friends, notably my brother Harold and Teddy Phillips, wrote stories and poems, and drew and painted to amuse themselves. Mervyn

Eltham College Rugby XV. Mervyn is top row, 2nd from left

already knew *Treasure Island* by heart, and could quote from any phrase onwards, and revelled at this stage in the poems of Masefield and Kipling. I wrote poems and had them published in the School Magazine (especially after I became Editor); and—in or out of class—read Shelley, Conrad, Shaw, Ibsen and Shakespeare, and sometimes 'Sapper'. . . . Leslie Peake, large, dark and kindly, and now Captain of Rugger, was known to have a large collection of Elizabethan dramatists in the Mermaid edition. The School produced *Hamlet* (with remarkable success), *Twelfth Night* (in which I played an unconvincing Antonio), and *King Lear*, the latter as an experiment with a middle-school cast and a fourteen-year-old hero. There were occasional visits to shows in London; we ran a camp at the School for East End Boys and their parents; and during the holidays there were other camps, and trips abroad, though I do not think that Mervyn accompanied any of these parties.

I had hoped to go up to Oxford, but my father had retired to a church in Bedfordshire and was desperately poor, so I had to defer these plans, and went instead, happily enough, to University College, London. My brother also left, but Mervyn stayed on at Eltham for a couple of years. He was well liked: for his extravagant sense of humour, the general air of piratical gusto he exuded, his notoriety as an artist, and, no doubt, because he was a pleasant and sympathetic person. His progress in his work remained moderate; but he had become a promising three-quarter, of the attacking type.

He invited me over to stay with him and his parents in Surrey, and later in Sussex, where his father had persuaded the Duke of Norfolk's Agents to let him build a cottage, 'Reed Thatch'. Soon we were inseparable friends. At school, three or four years' difference in age is a huge gulf, a caste-barrier; but as you grow older it becomes insignificant: you find you are contemporaries. Why our imaginations and dispositions fitted so amiably it is difficult to say. But we could meet after a month, and go on talking as if our conversation had never been interrupted.

Mervyn's days at Eltham were coming to a close. Though highly intelligent in so many ways, he was, as I have indicated, no academic. He had done well in Art and in English—though his spelling was never completely reliable when he was in a hurry. I shall not forget having to go right through the proofs of *Titus* again to alter the spelling of 'Fuchsia'. . . . But obviously his future lay in Art. So he left Eltham and went first to Croydon and then to the Royal Academy Schools.

As we were both in London, we saw more of each other than ever.

Art Student

I ONCE ASKED John Betjeman, whom I was showing round the
back streets of Taunton, whether he was familiar with the poems
of Mervyn Peake. He replied, rather tartly, 'Can he scan?'—which
I took to mean that he wasn't. But he would have liked the house
where Mervyn and his parents lived, at 55 Woodcote Road, Wallington. Dr. Peake, much in demand for maternity appointments
in that country-edge of suburbia, ran his practice there. I will not
swear that there was green and purple glass in the panels of the
front door, under the pillared porch, but I think there was: at
any rate there were stone mullions, and finials here and there;
and the general effect was comfortably pseudo-Gothic. The house
rambled three storeys high, and had a large garden with a croquet
lawn. For many years it was almost my second home.

In those days the professional classes still kept some domestic
staff: perhaps only a cook and a maid, who lived behind a green
baize door and had bedrooms at the top of the house. Such
arrangements were dying out; but at one stage Dr. Peake did have
occasion to engage a man-servant: and characteristically all the
male members of the Peake household (Leslie was now a chartered
accountant in the City) insisted that they must find one whose
surname was 'Jeeves'. Mrs. Peake said they were childish, but
(or so Mervyn maintained) they did find one. The gardener was,
unofficially, 'Tarzan', partly because of his mighty forearms, but
partly also because of his conversational style. On the other hand,
'Dotty Flies', the little man who helped with everything at their

cottage in Sussex, had always been called 'Dotty Flies' by local choice. I mention these harmless examples, not to enrage the class-conscious, but to suggest the private humours of a united family.

When you came into the hall, the drawing-room was on the right. This also served as a waiting-room for the surgery, and adjoined a conservatory which was filled in summer by the leaves of a gigantic vine. To the left of the hall was the dining-room. Here, in the morning, we would gather for breakfast. Mrs. Peake presided at one end of the table. At the other, her husband, deep-voiced and benign, bent his grey moustache and heavy brows over the task of exactly bisecting a grapefruit. Mervyn watched him intently, for it was a point of honour with the non-carver to choose the larger portion, if such could be distinguished. A false cut, and Mervyn would snatch, with a cry of triumph. Then his father would roll his eyes up to heaven, put down his knife, and demand loudly:

'*Oo*'s got the cheek of *a* 'orse?'

To which the rest of us would reply in ritual chorus:

'*Mervyn*'s got the cheek of *a* 'orse!' and Dr. Peake would snuffle happily to himself, while his wife smiled tolerant behind the coffee-pot.

In this house, among the stuffed pheasants from India and the chrysanthemums, and the engravings of the two Welsh squires who were said to be ancestors, Mervyn and I scribbled, and he drew and painted.

He had always been a great creator of monsters, even at school, fantastic creatures that took on an immediate life of their own. Some had long limp necks, some ears like a lynx, some pudgy toes, some incipient wings: but they were not merely amalgams, and their expressions hinted at deeper things. We decided that they were Mokuses (to rhyme with hocus-pocuses). I think I invented the term, but they were entirely his creations, and he himself used the spelling 'Mocus', or even 'Moccus'. Indeed, he made a collection of them later in *The Mocus Book*. But, at the time I have been talking about, we discovered, in our childish way, that they could be even more easily evoked if I first supplied a nonsensical name and a rhyme. For instance, I wrote:

4. Drawing of the Author (c. 1934)

Over the yellow plains of Ho
The hairy herds of Patti go,
With one before, and one behind,
Patti of most superior mind,
Who guard the others from their fate
And warily prognosticate.

or:

Until the Kingcups come again
The Arapooki is in pain:
So the Eurasian proverb runs—
Here are the Arapooki's sons.

or:

The Suba owns a hive of bees
And takes their honey when he needs it;
But, most, a Suba lives on cheese,
And that is how its Master feeds it.

And, suddenly, there they all were: the Patti, the Arapooki and his sons, the Suba, as well as the Maranesa, the Dusky Birron, the Pleeka, and half a hundred others. (Readers of *Peake's Progress* will perhaps have noted that the first half-dozen named above appear there). My rather long account here will help to explain references to Birrons and Subas and Pleekas in some of the letters from Mervyn which I quote later.

The Dusky Birron was a rather special case, for he became the hero of a book which we created together. We made up the story in consultation, as we went along; I did the actual writing of the story; and Mervyn supplied the map and the drawings. At one stage we called this fantastic tale *The Three Principalities*, but decided in the end that the proper title was *The Dusky Birron*. I remember discussing with him how the book should open.

'The best opening of any book in the world,' said Mervyn

5. *Rude Sketch* (c. 1933)

6. *The Author* (c. 1934)

firmly, 'is to *Moby Dick*: "Call me Ishmael".'

'Then we can't use that.'

In the end we began: 'So they marooned the Sailor-Man.' This was well in accord with Mervyn's *Treasure Island* mind. The Sailor-Man is a simple soul, a sort of childish prefiguring of the one in 'The Rhyme of the Flying Bomb' (surely the best English ballad-poem since the 'Ancient Mariner'?); and he is shown round the Island under the aegis of the Birron. The latter, as Mervyn's illustration shows him, is a sort of nude and bearded Wordsworth in gloves, but a creature of great courtesy and wisdom.

> The Dusky Birron may not die
> Because of movements in the sky.

The two travel around the Three Principalities, meeting many monsters. The first two states, Soz and Foon, are very grand (their respective mottoes are 'Semper Soz!' and 'Floreat Foon!'), but the third ('Cheerio Chee!') is more happy-go-lucky, and here our two companions come to a peaceful rest in the domain of the Suba.

After Chapman and Hall turned it down, we somehow never pursued the book into publication, though we always meant to. Mervyn's letters for several years are full of hopeful prophecies, and his brilliant drawings for it have appeared in various of his exhibitions, and (in part) in print. This is a pity, perhaps, since it is quite a good story, and we much enjoyed the making of it.

We had other schemes. Mervyn was anxious to do a series of articles for one of the London evening papers, to be called *Travels with a Zebra*. We were to acquire a beast of that species (how, it was not quite clear), and travel the English countryside. I would write the accounts (no doubt Stevensonian in style) of our explorations and of people's reactions, and he would do the illustrations. To Mervyn's disgust, the prosaic editor suggested that we should try a donkey. . . .

I have been writing about a rather loosely-defined period, before Leslie went out to Malaya, or Dr. and Mrs. Peake retired to 'Reed Thatch' beside the River Arun. It was a time of high hopes, tearing spirits and much activity. I wrote poems, some of which were published, and he drew and studied Art, and even played some rugger for the Old Boys' 1st XV, of which Mervyn's brother, a Billy Beaumont-like figure on the field, was Captain. Once the Kent County selectors even came down to watch Mervyn: but he became distracted by something at a critical moment during the match and lost his chance. . . .

We explored the wilds of Carshalton Park, experimenting with leaded throwing-sticks; talked incessantly, exchanging 'innocence for innocence'. He drove me among the hills of Surrey in the 'Scarlet Runner'. ('Mervyn, you ape, you've gone through the traffic-lights!') His letters were larded with monsters, edged with little scenes in Indian ink, bursting out into water-colour; full of schemes, invitations, literary and artistic pronouncements; with violent ruderies to shock my primness. One picked at random shows a sepia Pegasus with a pelican's head gazing at a sea-girt castle, and ends: '. . . I'd like to paint in Sark. Take your poems for Eric to see. O BOY, ISN'T LIFE GOOD!'

By this time Mervyn was, of course, a fully-fledged art student, having won a place in the Royal Academy Schools: and he revelled in the new persona. Picturesque figures were rarer then among the young, and the Press photographed him joyfully, in shaggy cords, bright loose tie, broad-brimmed hat and scarlet socks, with a canvas under his arm. Yet somehow, among the splendid talkers and bearded attitudinizers of Chelsea, he stood out as the genuine article. He had a rare sincerity, and one recognized that there was more here than mere talent.

It was for him, too, a time of growing independence, when he had to find his own code of morals and behaviour, preferably without hurting the feelings of his parents, of whom he was affectionately fond. Not that he was ever wild or ill-mannered, but 'le jeune homme fait ses expériences', and parents are often doubtful about their sons' first relationships, particularly with girls. Mrs. Peake, for some reason, thought I was a good influence on him: a notion about which Mervyn once expressed himself crisply! But in all her kind letters to me over the years she never hinted at any anxiety about his personal development.

It would be a mistake to think of his life at this time as being bounded by suburbia, with occasional excursions into Bohemian

Chelsea. Apart from 'writing sonnets in Crantock to a Cornish moon' (as he put it in a letter lazily dictated to his mother while painting 'on a 50 × 40 inch canvas for the Gold Medal'), and our Auvergne trip described at the beginning of this book, he had begun his long love-relationship with Sark.

We both went there first at the invitation of Eric Drake, who had returned from a year in the States with a young and attractive wife. Their plans to set up an artists' colony there were taking shape. Sark is, as those who have done more than go up the main track on a half-day visit know, a most romantic island. The coloured cliffs are so high and steep that you can only get in from the tiny entrance harbour by a tunnel; and all round its coastline are secret coves and bays, some with beaches and most of them obviously unvisited since you last broke a way down through the brambles a year ago. Though it is only a mile and a half long, and is divided almost into two by a high neck, you can be lost and alone in ten minutes, and can find a new place every day. The few inhabitants speak Norman French in their pubs, and drink the health of 'The Duke of Normandy'.

I remember scrambling with Mervyn across a steep cliff-face, with the waves smashing hungrily below. Somehow we got out to a knife-edge of rock that stuck out at right-angles from the face, like the branch-gable of a house. This we both straddled, and found ourselves gazing a bit anxiously up at the main cliff, which went up vertically, a few inches away, for another thirty or forty feet. The only hold seemed to be a shallow depression about half-way up. Perched on the top of the cliff, overhanging the edge, was a boulder about the size of a small cottage. I still do not know how we got up the face, though I remember getting first a knee and then a toe into the depression mentioned and reaching some sort of safety near the side of the boulder.

Mervyn also reached the top, but found himself on a tiny ledge just under the worst underhang of the boulder, with his arms clasping as much of its mass as he could compass. I edged towards him to help.

'If you come near me I'll bloody well kill you!' he muttered desperately.

Finally, by some contortion, he managed to turn himself right round, which was no comfort at all: for he was now facing outwards, looking down over the sea far below, with his arms spreadeagled behind him. All I could do was stay still, and watch. After long, agonizing minutes he inched his way to safety.

On a later occasion, when he spent many months alone on the island, he had a similar experience, only this time with a young cormorant in each coat pocket pecking angrily at his armpits as he hung. . . . This was the time when he found a long-stranded whale and cut out two of its vertebrae, which became familiar ornaments, sometimes supporting vases of flowers, in his various homes, and which appear in several of his paintings. Many of these happenings he described in *Mr. Pye*.

I have two oil paintings that he did in Sark. One of them he had kicked about the floors of his studios for years, till I objected. Several inches of the plaster-board had been broken off the top of the picture, but what I had framed was still about three feet by four. It is called *The Sea-Weed Gatherers*, and shows three men astride or kneeling on monstrous dappled horses amongst a shallow yellowish sea. The fronds of coloured weed they hold and admire have been found, and are, as he explained, poetry. In the far distance is an island, recognizably Sark.

The other painting is *Tintageoue* a sweep of bay with high rhubarb-coloured cliffs. He had gone out one day to the bay so named, to paint: only to discover that he had left all his brushes behind. So he did it all with his palette-knife, impasto.

After the War he was to return to Sark, as I tell in a later chapter, and he and Maeve rented a house there. The island became, one way and another, very much part of his mythological landscape.

Portrait of the Artist as a Young Man

I SHOULD MAKE some attempt to describe what Mervyn looked like, both in his early twenties and, with only minor changes, for many years afterwards—before he was prematurely aged by illness. No identikit in words can make up for one actual sighting, but I offer some physical facts, and some impressions.

He was tall, about six feet, though inclined to let himself become round-shouldered, particularly when crouched over a drawing. His hair was luxuriant and black, flowing back from a peak; and his eyebrows were heavily marked. There is a crude little sketch (if I could only find it) scratched by a rather drunken Dylan Thomas inside one corner of a publisher's dummy. It is just recognizably Mervyn, but the pencil has broken and left a rent in the paper, 'Oh Mervyn, I can *never* get your eyes deep enough! . . .'

Mervyn was, perhaps unexpectedly, rather a good mimic. He could put on a felt hat, adjust his reading-glasses, lose two feet in height, work his brows like a gorilla; and suddenly he was Groucho Marx, stepping far with bent knee behind his cigar, and muttering darkly, 'I have a compact with the flies: they don't practise Law; I don't walk on the ceiling!'

His mouth, normally wide enough, used to purse up as with a drawstring at moments of concentration or worry. When drawing, he held his stubs of pencil chimpanzee-wise, almost along, between the second and third fingers. His hands were long and sensitive, but not without knuckle; and the left one carried a silver ring set with a large, almost vulgar, green stone: a malachite which he had been given by a friend of Dr. Peake. This, he always maintained, was 'The Ring of the Peakes'; and with it he once inadvertently almost cut to pieces a man at a students' dance who made a foul remark about a girl.

He spoke pleasant and civilized English, without any trace of affectation, as those who met him or remember his broadcasts can confirm. A tall, dark fellow, then: good-looking enough; well-mannered, and active; to his friends, high-spirited and inventive; with a strong sense of fun, and for the absurd.

He had his social difficulties. 'I cannot imagine,' he once complained, 'what made me do it. Here was this Lady Whatsit, to whom I had been introduced, and a self-confessed art lover too: and she was talking the most arrant cock. So I nodded, and said "Yes",—and suddenly I found I was leaning over and had solemnly tapped the ash from my cigarette into the cup of coffee that she was in the course of drinking. . . . She immediately arose in high dudgeon, and left the room saying, "Really, the people one meets nowadays."'

When he was in more solemn mood he was, to make more modern comparisons, a bit like Tortelier conducting a master class on television, or Sir Michael Tippett looking for the truth beyond some intellectually plausible argument put forward by Bernard Levin. There was the same strong impact of sincerity.

But perhaps a more authentic impression of what he was like may be taken from some of the letters that he wrote at this time. These are always lively, warm-hearted and profusely illustrated in line or colour, and usually end 'Mervyn', 'Muffin', or even 'M. Leprosy Peake'. The two I give here, taken from many others almost at random, were both written from Wallington.

Hail Goaté!

Tons to tell you. Thanks awfully for letter. I'm a foul slacker not having written before. Say, I'm quite off the deep end about the Eric Drake scheme. Isn't it marvellous? Gosh! I'd give my soul to come. Pirates and octopi! O.K., Chief. I haven't heard anything from them myself, so of course I can't

7. *One of Mervyn's Pirates—*
The Lisping Lascar (1934)

write them or anything. From the Drakes, I mean, not the Octopi—now then, Mr. Jerome. . . .

Several of us, to be precise three, are holding a Show 'Au Chat Noir', Old Compton Street, Soho. We had a private view day, and had invitation cards sent to practically everybody of importance in the British Isles except you, including the Art Critics, they not being important but merely useful, Siegfried Sassoon, Philip of that ilk, Bernard Shaw, and McIver. A hundred cards were sent out; seven people of any import arrived, including Epstein. The great hit, however, was the Art Critic of the *News Chronicle*, which though a foul paper is widely read. He got Wallace Heaton, the Bond St. Photographers, to come down to the Show, and they took one of my pics. About my best to date.

I'm talking all about myself, as usual. I'm absolutely thrilled about the Sark biz. For goodness' sake write again soon and tell me more.

That's great about the Birron, Goaty. We'll make that blinking book a best-seller. Gee! don't worry. . . . Toy Birrons will be crowding out Woolworth's in 1932, while Marks and Spencers have sole copyright of Subas and Pleekas. . . . Lady Dillwater will lap it up, and turn on the bed-lamp at three in the morning to continue, when Lord D. is safely asleep. I've still about ten illustrations to do, you know.

Write tons of poetry. Sing songs and climb after walrus' eggs. . . . Count on me for Sark. Sark and the Birron indubitably go hand in hand, if not foot in foot.

> The Subas and the Pleekas are trying hard to live,
> But Octopi and Pirates are devils to forgive—
> And so we screamed with raptured joy, and climbed the
> > cliffs of Sark,
> While all the pebbles laughed at us, and glimmered
> > through the dark:
> Three tots of rum, a tentacle, two Erics and a shark.

I've decided to 'be' a Romanticist in Painting, but am going

8. Caribbean Pirate (1934)

to combine the guts of a Van Gogh with the design of a Puvis de Chavannes, and yet keep the suaveness of a Raphael running through stacks of corn that are yellower than yellow in the sunlight.

I have also worked out a scheme of super-imposing the drawing of an object upon the general, and most typical colour of the object. For instance, ivy is the coldish, bluish green, and a chestnut tree is a warming rich green. Let this most typical colour be painted broadly all over the object, and making either the tree's most typical shape, or the shape most fitting for the design. When the paint is dry, draw in the leaves in black or white or whatever colour suits the occasion, mood etc., very intricately, so combining broadness of vision with intricateness of expression.

. . . Have started the Gold Medal—*Echo and Narcissus*, 40–50-inch canvas—just think of the size. O Boy, it knocks you down at first sight. Now it's got the drawing all in, it looks half the size it did—

'O fat white canvas that nobody loves' . . . Damned expensive game this, you know.

It has come to this:

1. Sark is $a+$ —sheer Romance. Conrad talks bilge.
2. *The Dusky Birron* is a fortune-maker.
3. The Puis [*sic*] de Dôme country and round the Loire are the toppingest parts of the past.
4. Write again soon, in fact SOON.

Mervyn.

P.S. Doc. and Mrs. Doc. send their luff.

I give only a short extract from a second letter, which runs to eleven pages and is profusely illustrated with new monsters, Birrons' feet, and scarlet women:

Saturday, Feb. 13, 1932.
Wallington.
Hallo Goaty-Boy,

I have quite an amazing amount to tell you, so go back and eat your porridge first, or whatever you were going to do, and come back to the great, and it may even be immortal, letter when you have a free mind, and an expansive outlook.

I wrote you a week ago, when in the flush of success (for me), and forgot to post it. It ran thus:

'Am writing in the Wallington–Victoria express. Opposite me are two ill-natured women reading library books. You now have the setting. Do you realise that at the moment you are hanging in Wertheim's Gallery, Burlington Gardens, with *Annie Tompkins* and *The Chef*? They took all three and knocked out Doc. in the Panama hat. I have probably never had such a week in my life before. . .!'

The portrait of you is the most popular thing I've done. Freddy Crooke and Leslie Hurry are very keen on it. At the moment it is in Worthing, where the 'Twenties Group' has moved to. . . . Don't forget! You promised to be encumbered with it if it didn't sell. . . .

9. *A Group of Pirates* (c. 1936)

The Spoils of London

EVEN AFTER I went down from the University and Mervyn's parents retired from Wallington, we continued to meet regularly. He came to visit me at my various schools, or at Oxford when I went up to Oriel. We accompanied each other on holiday, to France, to Sark, to Sussex; or stayed at each other's homes. There were studios in Chelsea, or Battersea, or Kensington, which became familiar; and later, when he married, thanks to the friendship and generosity of Maeve, this companionship was enriched rather than curtailed.

As soon as my holidays began, we made arrangements to meet, usually in London. London was full of strange marvels; and was ours, from Tower Hill to Kew. Then as now, you could meet Tibetan lamas and see strange ducks in St. James's Park; and at Speakers' Corner an earnest man lectured (with diagrams) on the Foot-Writing of Apes: taking the Gorilla, the Chimpanzee and the Orang-Utan as corresponding to the three races sprung from the sons of Noah. The famous, and the poor, swam into and out of our ken. We explored the galleries, the book-shops, and the zoo. It was no credit to Mervyn's chivalry, nor to my supposed sense of humour, that when I wired him 'Meet me Small Cat House noon', he should have gone to wait outside the Women's Common Room of University College. . . .

From the tops of buses, from circuses, and foreign restaurants; out of a wild variety of lodgings and town houses and dance-halls, Mervyn took his spoils: little men with placards proclaiming 'The

End is Nigh!', waiters in sleazy bars, grotesque but pitiful women saying goodbye at railway termini to fantastic men, or the gazelles and rhinoceroses and eagles of Regent's Park. On an old envelope from his pocket or on a sketching-pad, he took them: strangely transformed, yet always real and convincing. I would pick them off the floor afterwards, to save them from trampling, hesitating only because I knew that, as like as not, he would say, 'Keep it, if you like it.'

Every walk became an expedition. 'Come!' Mervyn would say, 'I want to show you something.' And he would walk me all the way to some squalid in-flow of the Thames, where, bloated but half-sunk, a hundred thousand French letters floated down towards the sea. I was rather embarrassed, but Mervyn laughed his head off. 'Social comment!' he said.

Or, 'Come!' said Mervyn, as we were crossing Trafalgar Square: and he would take my elbow and steer me up the steps of the National Gallery, to stand below Uccello's huge painting of 'The Rout of San Romano'. 'There!' he would exclaim with childlike satisfaction, pointing to a recumbent figure in the bottom left-hand corner, 'The man who died in the cause of Perspective!'

We visited many contemporary exhibitions, of course, too; and other galleries, including the Tate. 'Ah!' he would say, pausing in tolerant wonderment before a Victorian conversation piece depicting a little girl restraining her over-exuberant puppy, and entitled—if I remember rightly—'Down, Pompey, Down!' Or he would sigh wistfully as he passed a picture by Augustus John, 'I wish I could paint only *one* head as *solid* as any of his!' Or he would ask, 'Do you remember those lantern-lectures at school, all about G. F. Watts?'

An appreciation of painting comes with more difficulty to the layman than the appreciation of poetry or music. He doesn't see enough examples, he comes with preconceptions about the subject-matter, and he has to learn to look at the picture itself. I shall always be grateful to Mervyn that I was made free of this world, not so much by precept as by shared enthusiasms and discovery.

Very occasionally, it was I who made the discovery. We had

10. *Match-Seller*

11. The Waiter

Picasso

12. *French-Style*

been looking at the Turners, and for some reason he hadn't been impressed. Perhaps he was thinking of facile reactions to a thousand copies of 'The Fighting Téméraire'. 'Look!' I objected. 'You're always talking about the qualities of the paint. Why not look at them for a moment just as patterns, like a rug, and then go on to the romantic subject-matter from there?' He grunted non-committally, and went on looking. After a few minutes he turned round to me again, amazed.

'You know,' he said, 'you're absolutely right! He's a great painter, a great poetic painter!' He could cherish a short-term prejudice, but he was always too honest not to find a better truth.

Indeed, his eye for quality was acute. Coming out of a narrow alley off Bond Street one day, he caught sight of a coloured drawing, one of a dozen stuck in the glass door of a shop across the road. 'Wait a bit!' he exclaimed, and went across to see. . . . It proved to be an original Daumier, unrecognized and going for a few pounds.

So he stalked through London, a picturesque figure, seeking his prey. He met many odd people in his wanderings, and could talk familiarly, and sympathize, with them all. In his poem, 'The Cocky Walkers', he sees the teenage drop-outs lined by their 'cold familiar wall' with terrible clarity, but what he appreciates and understands also is their independence, and the 'sap' in their young growth. When he talked with an old lady on the train at Croydon and she told him, 'You see, I am quite alone: it is terrible to be lonely!' he was troubled by it for weeks, and wrote about it, in another poem.

One night he was invited out to dinner by a chance acquaintance. His host proved to be a rich young man, and they dined alone at his house in some luxury. Then, to Mervyn's horror and embarrassment, his host began to speak of friendship and its great possibilities of extension, between those of the same sex. . . . He told me about it afterwards. He was still very upset.

'What happened?' I asked.

'Oh, well, then he tried to embrace me, and I hit him. It was awful!'

Pratt

13. *The Man in the Cap* (c. 1934)

'Any difficulty?'

'No, it wasn't that. I just walked out. But as I left I could hear him crying, weeping as if his heart was broken.'

On another occasion, he had what seems to have been a quite impersonally clinical conversation with a male pimp about the physical disadvantages and actual pains of his profession. Mervyn could have said, with Terence, *humani nil a me alienum puto*.

But all his encounters were not with such tragic or shadowy figures. I was with him one day, somewhere near Ebury Street, when he stated, 'There's a new poet. He lives round about here, and we must go and see him.'

'Why must we?'

'Because he's terrific. T. S. Eliot says so, in a review of his first book. It's called *Nine Poems*, or *Ten Poems*, or something.'

'Obviously an economical fellow!'

'The point is,' said Mervyn earnestly, 'he's dying. Of consumption, like Keats. He lies in bed and drinks beer, they say, and eats nothing but wedding-cake.'

'They'll say anything. I don't believe a word of it. What's his name?'

Mervyn thought for a moment. 'Er, Thomas, I think. That's right. Dylan Thomas.'

It rang no bells. 'Another bloody Welshman,' I suggested.

Mervyn shook his finger at me. 'When you say that, you insult me too! All Englishmen are flat and bourgeois. All Scotsmen are entirely lacking in imagination. Like Sir Walter Scott—' (This was an old quarrel between us, but before I could interrupt to remind him that he hadn't actually read Sir Walter Scott, he had swept on.) 'But Welshmen are the salt of the earth!'

'That may be,' I conceded, 'though I was bitten by one once, in a rugger match at Ebbw Vale. Nevertheless, I am not going to intrude on a dying poet, just because he lives near Ebury Street, wedding-cake or no wedding-cake!'

As it happened, we did not have to intrude upon a dying poet, for by some curious chance we met him that very evening. It was at one of those Chelsea parties where you find yourself somehow. He didn't appear to be dying. Indeed, anything less like the

14. Middle European (c. 1934)

popular conception of Dylan Thomas it would be hard to imagine. He was a remarkably handsome, slim, and faun-like young man, who spoke beautiful English, and exuded charm. Characteristically, perhaps, he smoked all the tobacco I had left in my pouch.

I did not see a great deal of him after that meeting, but he became a regular acquaintance of Mervyn's, and would drop in unexpectedly at his studio, usually drunk and homeless, to be sick on the floor and then spend the night on the couch. Though he retained a good deal of charm, and (Mervyn assured me) wrote poetry only when he was stone-cold sober, there is no doubt that—apart from anything else—he grew more conceited as he grew older and more famous.

Mervyn's meeting with another poet is related in a letter which he sent me, adorned with a lively little sketch of the subject:

Sunday, October 18th, 1936.
Goaty-Boy,

Thanks for p.c.s. Don't feel you've got to get that done by any particular time. Rushing it won't help it. Sooner the better, however. How are things? Wish you were down here now.

I've been getting my foot into the *London Mercury*'s door. Am dining with the Editor next wk!!!?!!!

Drew Stephen Spender on Thursday. Do you like his stuff? Some of it is really grand. I think I never read it before. . . .

Most beautiful person I've met. Utterly Byron and Shelley rolled into one. I was thunderstruck. I thought they only existed in novels, these ivory poets.

However, I'll send you a print when it comes out. Probably next month.

Ever yrs.
Mervyn

Other well-known figures came his way through this series of drawings for *The London Mercury*. One of the most charming of these was Walter de la Mare. I never met him, but Mervyn put us in touch, and for some time we exchanged an enjoyable

15. Café Anglais, Soho (c. 1934)

16. *London Wide Boy (Oct 1938)*   17. *Reclining Model (1936)*

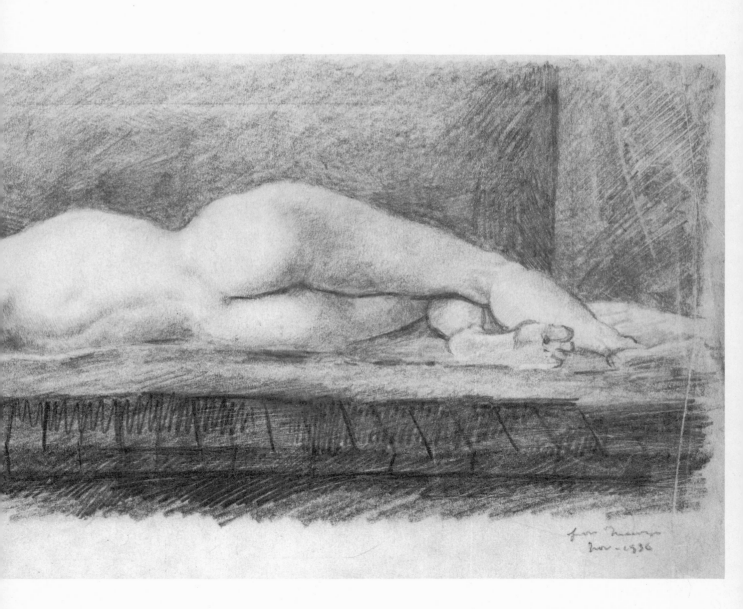

correspondence on children's poetry, and on creative imagination generally: subjects in which we were both interested and which formed part of the work for my doctorate at Oxford.

A briefer meeting was with Roy Campbell. Mervyn met him in 'The World's End', drunk and rather sorry for himself, perhaps uncharacteristically. 'I know,' he said tearfully, 'I'm only a tum-tum poet; only a tum-tum poet. . . .'

A close and very helpful friend of Mervyn's from quite early days was Lady Moray. We went to the theatre with her on various memorable occasions, and she was a charming hostess: though you never quite knew whom you might meet. I remember her remarking that it was a pity Betty couldn't come to tea after all, as she had a cold, and suddenly realizing that she was speaking of the (then) Duchess of York; also, talking to a little girl in a vaguely familiar tartan, who asked, 'Uncle Goaty, are you coming to stay with us at Dunsinane, too?. . .'

Nor have I forgotten the Golden Hamster of Pont Street, though I met this animal some years later than the events recounted in the present chapter. It seemed an amiable beast, and went to sleep on my best overcoat; but when I went out again into the bitter London streets I could not understand why my back was so cold—till I discovered that a whole square foot of material had been devoured. . . . Mervyn was highly amused.

About this time, shortly before the War, Mervyn made a tinted drawing (here reproduced), which he called 'The Beggars are Coming to Town!' It shows a ragged train of his friends, including Leslie Hurry, Freddie Crooke, Tony Bridge (I think), and myself. But there is also a haunting new face, in a significant position, among the beggars: that of Maeve, his wife.

He met her when he was teaching at the Westminster School of Art. Maeve Gilmore was the daughter of an Irish doctor and his wife, and had been convent-educated. It was near the Serpentine, one evening, that he told me about her. At first I was rudely sceptical.

'What, again?'

'No. It's really serious this time. Honestly.'

'You're sure?'

*18. 'The Beggars are Coming to Town'. Among the beggars are Maeve (centre right), with
Mervyn behind her, partly obscured by the branch, and the author (centre left, immediately to the right of the stick).*

19. *Young Maeve (1938)*

'Yes.'

'Well, good luck to you. Does she like you?'

'I hope so,' said Mervyn humbly. 'I think so.'

And from his letters, it was clear that he was really in love.

He has drawn and painted her, and described her in his poems: a slim, beautiful girl with a helmet of golden hair and dark eyebrows. She spoke precise English in a light, gentle voice, and had a Madonna-like composure, outwardly at least, that took her through all occasions; but behind this lurked a sense of humour, which was sometimes even (to Mervyn's great satisfaction) quite earthy.

One of the shows we went to see together was *The Insect Play*, for which Mervyn had produced some remarkable costumes; and his hopes were high, as always, that this might be the beginning of greater things. Financially, the greater things were slow to come; but his proclivity towards odd encounters persisted.

It was, I think, shortly after they became engaged that we went to see John Gielgud in the part of Richard the Second. Mervyn was to draw him, as part of his *London Mercury* series, but Gielgud had sent him a note saying that his dressing-room was too small for the purpose, and suggesting that the drawing might be done from a stage-box. Accordingly, he and Maeve and I found ourselves ensconced in one in great luxury, while Gielgud postured helpfully to display his striking profile only a few feet away. Mervyn drew his nose very carefully, but after that he became interested in the play, and had to complete the portrait later from memory and with the aid of photographs! In fact, it was an excellent likeness.

What particularly remains in my mind about that evening, however, was not the drawing. Looking down from our box into the stalls between scenes, I had noticed the unmistakable figure of Mr. Winston Churchill (as he then was) sitting in the second row beside his wife. When the interval came, I retired to the room labelled 'Gentlemen', and was standing there thoughtfully going about my business when a bulky personage arrived to stand beside me. He took far longer than I did, and I came out into the corridor to find my companions. They were not about, but Mrs. Churchill was there, waiting, and she asked me if I could supply a light for her cigarette. She was very charming, and we had just begun talking when I was almost hurled bodily against the wall. . . . Her husband had emerged, to take her arm and sweep her away down the passage. She apologized pleasantly over her shoulder; and for some reason I felt no resentment at all.

Mervyn and Maeve were married at St. James's, Spanish Place. It was an impressive occasion, with a red carpet and awnings and fine ceremonial. I was Best Man, and managed to bring Mervyn, looking dogged and somehow rather sinister in his black hat and morning coat, to his place in the church in time. Before the rich vestments and the lustrations of the officiating clergy, he must have felt himself lost in a strange and formal world, for he muttered, 'Don't you *dare* to genuflect!' But we did.

Over thirty years of married life, of long happiness and final tragedy, but always of mutual love and devotion, lay before them.

A strange adventure befell them shortly before their honeymoon, the sort of thing that could only happen to Mervyn. He and Maeve told the story in a broadcast interview. One evening, after retiring to Mervyn's first-floor studio in Battersea, they were disturbed by unusual noises, coming apparently from under the rug in front of the fireplace. When they took the rug away, they uncovered a trap-door; and when this was prised open they found themselves looking down upon . . . the back of an elephant! They spent the rest of the evening feeding it with bits of bread or lumps of sugar. No obvious subsequent explanation (of a circus being accommodated for the night in the ground-floor warehouse) could take away from so characteristic an experience. Mervyn was always elephant-prone.

Neither at this time nor later, of course, were their lives or habitations confined to London. There was Sark again, which we all three visited and where they were afterwards to live; there were the cottages at Burpham and Wepham, near Arundel in Sussex; they went on a miniature 'Grand Tour' with Mrs. Gilmore shortly before their marriage which included the baroque splendours of Prague, and Hungary. Later, Yugoslavia and Spain were visited.

20. *Maeve*

In Yugoslavia Mervyn had occasion to take a bath. The hotel was proud of its fine new bathroom, where he ran the water, threw his clothes as usual on the floor, and got in to wallow in the warmth. When he had finished, he pulled the plug out with his toe, and continued to lie there while the bath emptied. 'Then suddenly,' he said, telling me the story, 'out of the corner of my eye, I saw something moving. It was my clothes. They were moving. In fact, they were floating across the floor. . . . I leapt out of the bath. There was water everywhere, going under the door, cataracting down the stairs. . . . There were muffled cries coming up from below—'

'What *is* all this? How come?'

'Well, you see, there was this nice new bath, standing on its four little legs, with taps and plug and everything handsome. But no one had troubled to connect up any plumbing with the outflow: the hole in the bath simply let the water out on to the plain floor a few inches below it. No doubt they intended to get round to it later.'

London, however, was always their real base. In *A World Away*, her moving account of their life together, Maeve has told something of their problems and adventures at this period, though she writes even more fully of later times, during and after the War. On one point only I would venture to qualify what she says. She speaks of her own shyness, when she first married, and of what she suggests was her inefficiency as a young wife, especially on social occasions. I am sure she did feel shyness sometimes, and found difficulties of adjustment: nevertheless the description of herself as so tremulous a flower is misleading. She left a very different impression on others. Pre-eminently, she 'coped'. Serene, carrying her cat Tchaka perhaps, she could provide a meal at the shortest notice, or grace a social occasion with composure and charm. She wrestled magically with acute financial problems for years: just as she found time to paint with distinction, brought up a family on a lonely island, attended a tragically failing husband with courage and devotion, and, after his death, fought to secure him juster recognition.

Much of what Mervyn was writing in the late 1930s did not

21. *Maeve on Sofa*

appear till later, and then perhaps only in limited wartime editions on poor paper. Some of his best poetry, the beginnings of *Gormenghast*, and *Captain Slaughterboard Drops Anchor* were all on the stocks.

I have a special fondness for the last of these works. It is a happy piece of sheer exuberance, by an expert on pirates. But I also have a personal interest, since I figure, next to Dr. Peake, tattooed on the back of the pirate captain's neck; and since, when Mervyn was stuck for a suitable ending, I was able to give him the idea. But while the main figure of the book is obviously a sort of self-dramatization, it has hardly been noticed that the Yellow Creature also has a human counterpart, or at least a partial identification. Though hardly beautiful, or even feminine; though more companion and faithful attendant than lover or wife; the Yellow Creature is just recognizable, at moments, even by some detail of feature. . . . An affectionate transmogrification.

22. Model in Profile

23. Maeve Knitting (Nov 1939)

The Coming of the War

On 3 September 1939, Mervyn and Maeve were visiting me and my family in Chipping Campden. Maeve was expecting her first child a few months later. We were all rather serious. The War had been a long time coming, its irruption dependent upon a madman's whim; and we all expected sudden and perhaps complete destruction.

It is possible to take too simplistic a view of Mervyn Peake's career: cheerful youth culminating in a happy marriage; the stress of War ending in breakdown; and finally long illness and death. Clearly there is some justice in this division; and the facts may be read in Maeve's poignant book and in John Watney's biography. But it should be remembered that the War years and the years following produced much of his best work, and that there were happiness and enthusiasm long persisting. Looking back, I remember him as very much the same Mervyn, for all his troubles, till near the very end.

Mervyn was a completely non-political animal. If he was a rebel it was not against the Establishment. But he was by nature the world's worst soldier. He had hoped to use his talents as an official war artist, but though his sponsors included at various times Sir Kenneth Clark, Sir Edward Marsh, Augustus John and Epstein, it was not till much later that he was sent out to Germany to draw. As Gunner Peake, and Sapper Peake, he suffered in an alien world. What he felt, bound by (to him) meaningless restrictions, among companions who shared none of his interests, is vividly

24. *Pensive* (c. 1939)

told in one of the letters given below. At the end of one leave, when I was accompanying him on his way, he swung round suddenly and said desperately, 'You know, Goaty, there's only you now: you're almost my only friend!'—and strode off into the darkness. The confession was unwonted, and no doubt exaggerated, but it shows how lonely he felt.

In the end there was a breakdown. As he described it to me, it was something of a 'Sam, Sam, pick oop thy moosket!' affair, though none the less tragic for that. 'I bent down to do up my boot-lace,' he explained, 'when I suddenly realized that I could never obey another order again, not ever in my whole life!'

But, as I have said, his experiences, and feelings, and changes of mood, are better expressed in his letters. Some of these are of quite unusual interest and importance. The first one I quote is, however, only incidentally concerned with the War. It is dated (by the date-stamp on the envelope) 6 October 1939, and came from the house in Sussex to which his parents had retired.

Reed Thatch,
Burpham, Arundel,
Sussex.

Dear Goaty,

I am writing to tell you about Mother, who I am afraid has not long to live now. Maeve came up from Stratford and she and I are now with Doc. down here. We have been here about three days, and Doc. had no idea that she could still have been alive now. She is frightfully weak and the paralysis has now attacked her face and jaw, so that she cannot talk or swallow. It's terribly tragic. In a way we are all hoping that she will pass away now and not have to go on suffering, when there is no hope. She is frightfully brave and tries to smile when she can, but fortunately is unconscious a lot of the time.

I wanted to let you know because I know you were very fond of her and she was of you. Not that one can do anything. That's what's so awful.

Cheerio, Goaty. It's nice having someone to write to. Thank heavens for Maeve too.

Sir Kenneth Clark came over (to 49) and carried away eighteen guineas' worth of drawings a week ago. Frightfully keen on them. All the best of luck.
Yours ever
Mervyn.

The next letter I give is dated 17 November 1940, and is written round a pen-sketch of a centaur with his arms clasped back over his head. After some general preliminaries, he goes on:

. . . Your letters come like a draft (*sic*) of fresh air into this khaki prison of a life. Are you pleased with your job? How are things? Fancy being down in the wild West like that. Lancashire stinks, and Blackpool, I imagine, is Lancashire's finest example of a cess-pit. One thing only is good here. I went up a marble stair-case, paying 8d. at the door, and after pushing through a flock of Commissionaires I found the finest example of a lion that I have ever seen. Apparently I was in a Zoo. There were also hyenas, bears, lynxes, pumas, monkeys, etc. The lion inspired me to write this. Is it any good?

> In the lion's yellow eyes
> Floats the grief of dynasties
> Floats the pain of Emperors
> Dying under tragic stars.
> In the lion's eyes I see
> The yellow lake of prophecy;
> While the fickle gods of war
> Tell me what I'm needed for,
> In the lion's eyes I read
> Of what it is I am and need.

By the way, my address is 62 Coronation Street, Blackpool, Lancs. 'Come up and see me sometime!'
Seriously though, I would give away my entrails for a talk with you. Two pipes. A fire. And the night ahead.
Will those days come again?

Puille

25. *Palais de Danse (1940)*

I am trying to write and draw. Everything seems to have fallen through that I had banked on. War Artist's job, etc. I've written seventeen chapters of GORMENGHAST. Do you remember Lord Groan, etc.? I spouted two chapters to you long ago in a place called Warning Camp.

Have you much time for yourself? If you get any ideas that are illustrable I've time here to do them. What about finding our stuff selling like mad when the War's over? Maeve and Sebastian have come to B'pool, which is marvellous. Arundel had a lot of bombs, and anyway the chance of 'sleeping out' was too good to be missed. She sends undiluted love to you, and x.x.x.x.'s. Oh Goaty Boy, my one and only Suba. Believe me when I say it *is* Subas that matter.

Write again.

Mervyn

26. *Soldiers (1940)*

But the next letter I have chosen, dated 7 March 1942, shows even more tension and unhappiness.

Sapper Peake 1597577
No 1 T.B., R.E.
Lowmoor Mill
Clitheroe, Lancashire.

Navel, my old cock! Do you still seethe with mobile leprosy? Do you still enjoy scratching at your silt-sluiced belly? . . . Are you still free of the Army— I *do* hope so—and long may you remain so if you are. Oh God, I'm sick, sick, sick of it—the perpetual littleness of the life—the monotonous conversation of what I suppose are my comrades who are with me polishing buttons and blancoing the webbing in our fight against world tyranny. If I sound bitter it's because I'm afraid I am, rather— they've done nothing but muck me about from unit to unit. Granted, I'm hopeless, but I wouldn't be if they'd put me into something where my talent could be used. No wonder we're doing badly in the war. If they put the wrong people in the wrong jobs at the bum-end of the army they probably do the same at the scalp end.

I've been meaning to write to you many times. It's with a great sense of nostalgia that I do so—nostalgia for our conversation and sympathy with each other's outlook and some weird tie which we have and which I am jealous of. There is no one I'd rather see than you. I am in a little village in Yorkshire. It's raining like hell. It's Sunday. I got away from the barracks where I've just been sent from London (old cotton mill we're in) . . . I got away early hoping for a long walk over the moors and the rain has started water-falling down, Tried one dark pub—wouldn't give me lunch, dirty woman, black skinny cat with her—no milk of human kindness (probably the cat had it). But a mile further on, got here. Fire, big room, milk-of-human-kindness woman and hellish homesickness for warless days. Why don't you shove your head through the window? I've got a lot of tobacco, and over the last ten years I must by now be owing you 10000000^9 ozs.

27. *Soldier Asleep (1940)*

28. *Soldiers Sparring (c. 1942)*

Shapes and Sounds selling very well. 500 up to date, which for poetry is remarkably good (my publishers tell me—what!). Sounds a bit up-stage, doesn't it?—'my publishers'. Ha ha. Sorry—I'm going a bit weird.

We don't know where Leslie is. We hope he got away from Singapore, but they caught such a lot, didn't they? Ruth and the kids got to Australia, thank God. Not that that is too safe.

I don't know what I'd do if I heard that he'd been killed. I just want to cry when I think of the stupidity of the whole bloody, ghastly, sordid business.

Doc's O.K. and little Maeve. I saw her about ten days ago, before they cattle'd one up here. We talked of how we'd love to see you again. Sebastian loved his card from you, and Maeve was so pleased.

Take care of yourself and write again soon.

Mervyn

29. Blitzed Hangar at Biggin Hill
(1941)

This was perhaps the unhappiest letter I ever received from him. Much later, after the War, when he became seriously ill, he was always gentle and uncomplaining; while a letter I received after his temporary breakdown shows far more composure:

Ward N. Southport Emergency Hospital.
Southport, Lancs.
Catfish,

About 1027000 years ago I had a letter from you in a place called Clitheroe. It was a goodly, if not a godly letter—a letter that ranks among your better ones, an *a*— at least: and an inconceivable thing occurred. *I started to answer it on the day I got it.* . . . I have lost my two-page hot-on-the-heels letter and the bloody days, hours, months have dribbled away . . . Knowing you to be practically the bloodiest correspondent in the world in your own right, I feel fairly confident that you'll merely shrug a leprous shoulder at the memory of my long silence and outbalance it by recalling a bamboo cane with a hunk of lead at one end which we threw across five fields and a lake or two to one another in golden days.

This address'll surprise you but nothing dramatic happened, either the loss of a head or even the tiniest, weeniest, dinkyest twitch of flesh—and Southport ladies look lovingly at me until they find I wasn't wounded at Dunkirk. For we are very noticeable in this artificial town with its sea on the horizon, for we are draped in shapeless 'suits' of peacock blue with crimson rag ties, and, oh f—k.

No, just a nervous collapse suddenly with the usual symptoms—sleeplessness at night and tired all day (ironically)—irritable as a bereaved rattle-snake and apt to weep on breaking a bootlace. Whipped here at high speed and have been here since May.

With luck will be home within a fortnight and getting a job at the M.O.I. I wish you were in London. Any chance of seeing you? O, I hope so.

New anthology, *Poetry in Wartime* (Fabers) just out. . . . Vernon Watkins, very good, I think. . . . I want to see what

you've written. . . . I think I've gone ahead in my literary consciousness and have a kind of grip on things more than I had and wouldn't be quite so woolly now if we could burn the midnight oil.

My chief problem is one of Form, and I find myself to be expressing things overmuch in the five-beat line, irrespective of the core of the notion. Not really quite as bad as that, but a lack of being able to leap instinctively into the *only* form that the [*erased*] mood must be externalised by. I want my poems to create this form in a *growth* way, out of the very nature of the thought, unfolding as they continue from line to line, from idea to idea, and then to close in gradually (or swiftly) like the petal of a flower at night . . .

Tell me what time you have off in Sept. . . . If you turn up I'll teach you how to play a pipe. It's the most thrilly thing in the world. There's bribery for you! I have made two pipes now, one in A and one in D, and can play simple tunes. The plaintive, woody, reedy, dryad timbre of the things tears the souls (*sic*) off your feet. The making of them is . . . exciting. Bamboo is the best thing to make them of, though I want to make one of black walnut: brace-and-bit(ing) it right through (one inch diameter) and then cutting away, rasping, etc., until I have a perfect tube, very slender. I had to learn the very simplest things before I could get going, for I couldn't read a line of music, and semibreves, minims, crotchets, quavers, etc., might have been the names of lost tribes for all I knew.

. . . I've got to illustrate 'The Ancient Mariner' for Chatto's now, and a book for Joad called *The Young Soldier in Search of a Better World* somewhat paralleling Shaw's *Black Girl*, etc.

Haven't been able to do a thing here, been so jittery. Thank Gog, I'm much better. . . . Take care of yourself—

Mervyn

Mervyn with Sebastian at Burpham, c. *1942*

I got up to London as soon as I could. My only military duties were in the Home Guard. (The Bishop of Truro—a keen member—and I used to keep watch over the midnight pubs of Cornwall.) There was no difficulty about missing parades, so when the school holidays came I went up to see Mervyn, who had, as he mentioned above, obtained a post with the Ministry of Information.

He was just changing digs, and had been staying either at the new digs or with Maeve, I forget which; but it was quite early in the morning that we went back to his old place (which was somewhere near Chenies Street), to pick up the last of his things. The University of London building, which the Ministry then occupied, was only two minutes down the road.

When we got to the house, our attention was caught by a long panel of inscriptions, scribbled down a blank space to the left of the outside door. They were by Professor Joad, then a well-known broadcaster. The top one, politely written, said,

'Dear Mervyn, I wonder if I could see you about the drawings, which are now over-due? Yours, C.E.M.J.'

Below that was scrawled,

'Called again yesterday. Please let me have drawings, *soon*. C.E.M.J.'

The fifth and sixth messages, down at the bottom, were both curt and frantic.

'Oh, Lord!' said Mervyn penitently, 'I swore I'd let him have those drawings a week ago, and I've not done one of them yet!' Fortunately, he was a remarkably fast worker when he put his mind to it.

We went in and upstairs to Mervyn's room, where we packed up the remains of his gear. How a jar of plum jam (broken) came to be under his pillow, with his pyjamas, neither of us could imagine.

We went downstairs, and piled the luggage in the hall. It was still quite early morning. Mervyn seemed in good spirits. 'What about some breakfast?' he suggested.

'Good idea. Where?'

'Let's go to the Ministry. They do quite a good breakfast there.'

'Wouldn't I need a pass, or something? I mean, it's where all the secrets of the war effort are stored, isn't it? I don't want to be shot as a spy.' Down the road I could see the coils of barbed wire and the glint of bayonets as the sentries turned. 'Tight security, I imagine.'

'A modicum. A mere modicum perhaps,' said Mervyn airily. 'Not a plethora. Don't *worry* so! Leave it all to me.'

He sidled past the sentries and into the front hall, where there were Commissionaires with medal-ribbons and forbidding-looking men behind a counter. He walked over to a rack containing forms. They were applications for admission. We were required to establish our identities, say whom we wished to see, and state our business.

'I think I shall put "Propaganda for the Poles",' said Mervyn thoughtfully. 'That's what I think *I* make.' I peered over his shoulder as he stood there, pencil poised, expecting personally to be arrested at any moment. In the end, he wrote nothing at all. Instead, he drew a very small elephant with a very large navel; and this he waved cheerfully at all and sundry as he led me inside. . . .

As he had promised, we had an excellent breakfast.

In spite of his present cheerfulness, he had been naturally worried after his breakdown in the North, and at his request I had put him in touch with Dr. William Brown, an eminent psychiatrist, who had been one of my supervisors at Oxford. Mervyn wrote an amusing account of the interview:

'. . . Your letter proved invaluable. I've seen Dr. Brown, who impressed me very much. There he was, at the far end of the consulting room, about the size of a halma man. After walking for some time across the Harley carpet, he grew taller and taller, until at last (about 4.15) I got a close-up of him. "I am delighted to do anything I can for a friend of Dr. Smith's," he said.'

I do not think that Dr. Brown, who was certainly an Imposing

Figure ('Like a great eagle,' said Mervyn), did anything to help him with his personal problems, on one visit, but he was enormously influential, and may have helped to secure him more relevant consideration later. At any rate, it was kind of him.

The War had still well over a year to run, and I could continue quoting from Mervyn's letters and recounting anecdotes or conversations. I remember his telling me how he probably burned down part of the Duke of York's Barracks. (*The Court*: 'You have admitted that you were in the habit of throwing your cigarettes into the waste-paper bin. Would you agree that it was possibly your cigarette-end which was responsible for the fire?' *Mervyn*: 'Possible, yes sir.' *The Court*: 'Would you not further agree that it was *probably* responsible for the fire?' *Mervyn*: 'No, sir. Possible, but not probable.') The case was non-proven, as the Scots say.

I have vivid recollections of staying with him in London, when the V2s crashed among the neighbouring streets, and the V1s, the 'doodle-bugs', buzzed ominously overhead, and then cut out, above the glass roof of the studio. Then you counted carefully up to seventeen, wondering if you would be alive at the end of that time, for the things always seemed to be coming right down the back of your neck. . . .

I recall more hopeful letters from him, and from Maeve, with invitations to stay in Sussex. Later still, he told me a little of his horrifying visit to a newly-'liberated' Belsen, a visit that he recorded memorably in drawings (see pages 122–24) and in poetry, and one that left a deepening wound.

But more and more it was his work: his book illustrations, his poems, and his progress in the composition of the volume he called *Groan*, which became dominant; and in the next chapter I say something about their making. This is not a critical study, and I am mainly concerned with personal observations; but his letters in particular do throw valuable light on his intentions. Some of the ones I shall cite were written as early as 1943, and could therefore have been included in this chapter: but the last years of the War and the years following merge, as a time of considerable achievement, and—in this loosely chronological survey—I have considered them together.

31. *Ten Consecutive Studies of Maeve, each drawn in less than a minute*

Achievements

No part of Mervyn Peake's work has received less adequate recognition than his poetry. The recent publication of *Peake's Progress,* a volume that contains not only a selection of his shorter poems but also two important longer pieces, 'The Rhyme of the Flying Bomb' and 'A Reverie of Bone', may perhaps do something to hasten a juster appreciation. His brilliance as an illustrative artist, and the imaginative power of the 'Gormenghast' trilogy, have distracted attention from what may well be accepted as an achievement of at least equal value.

His early poems were pleasant and colourful but derivative, at first from Kipling, Masefield and similar writers; and, though always sensitive and observant, suffered from conventional form. The letter quoted in a previous chapter shows how he was seeking to find 'an inevitable' form growing out of the subject and intention; and this effort, combined with the utter sincerity of his approach, began to produce a remarkable new development of style. I had been enjoying his poems, almost as they were written, for years: and now suddenly realized, almost as it were overnight, that he had become an important modern poet.

It was when I read 'Rhondda Valley', I think, that I first recognized this new quality. The publication of *Shapes and Sounds* confirmed me in my opinion. The title is interesting. It is not 'Pictures and Colours', as a painter's book might have been called, and the shapes and sounds are not those of the subject-matter only. They are the shapes and sounds of the poems, which, for

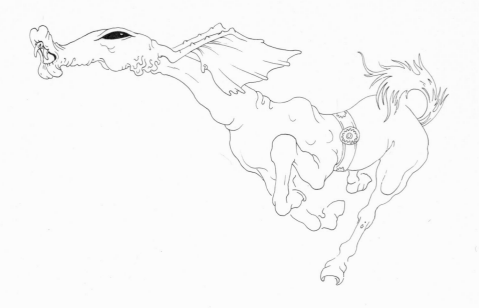

32. *Flying Horse. Preliminary sketch for illustration of Maurice Collis's* Quest for Sita, *an oriental fantasy published in 1946*

33. *In the Pub*

34. *At the Bar*

all their vivid imagery, are not primarily descriptive. They are translucent and relevant not to a painter's achievement, but to a poet's.

There *are* striking images everywhere, of course, as in his 'Cocky Walkers', where he tells of

> . . . the flash boys, uncaught,
> Treading the reedy springboard of green days

or, from the title-poem,

> . . . when a great
> And gull-winged Bible in a sudden draught
> Rustles its sacred pages and the naves
> Whisper of how a midnight leaf of *Amos*
> Is lifting in the darkness, or of a gust
> Rattles the sheets of *Jonah*.

But he was not a 'literary' writer, like Tennyson, who knew how words would behave for him. He had to discover words (hunting even in Roget's *Thesaurus* for his treasure), and find out what the poem itself demanded as it grew. Of course, during composition, the words came spontaneously, or seemed to; and sometimes a phrase came first, fully-fledged. 'Swan arrogant!' he said to himself, walking by the River Arun, and the poem of that name was almost made.

He dedicated his second volume of poems, *The Glassblowers*, to me—a distinction I much appreciated. It includes 'The Consumptive. Belsen, 1945', and some fine love-poems to Maeve. (His touching 'The Slender Gazelle', to her, had already been chosen by Walter de la Mare for his anthology *Love* in 1943.)

I have already praised 'The Rhyme of the Flying Bomb' as one of the great ballad-poems. The main figure here has obvious antecedents ('Pirate Peake', *Treasure Island*, the Sailorman in *The Dusky Birron*, and *Captain Slaughterboard*), but they have all been transmuted by compassion and imagination. The poem, one of the most important to come out of the Second World War, celebrates the whole destruction of London, even more strikingly than his earlier 'London 1941', 'half-masonry, half-pain'.

35. Woman in Café (1941)

'A Reverie of Bone' had been long in composition and under constant revision. He used to read me extracts over a period that must have spanned ten years. It is full of pictorial images of remarkable power, and its imaginative approach belongs more nearly to the world of Gormenghast than that of any of his other poems.

It is for his drawings and his book illustrations that many people most value Mervyn Peake. He was a brilliant draughtsman, as his sketches of his children, his formal life-studies, or his drawing of a baby in John Brophy's *The Human Face* serve to remind us. But all the thousands of his drawings are touched with his individual imagination. There is no mistaking the authorship of a Peake drawing.

His book illustrations fall into several groups. There are his own original creations, like *Captain Slaughterboard Drops Anchor* or *Letters from a Lost Uncle*; there are books like *Treasure Island*, *Alice in Wonderland* and *The Hunting of the Snark*, which were all long familiar and particularly 'sib' to his imagination; and there are collections almost as much to hand, like *Ride a Cock-Horse* and *Grimm's Household Tales*. All these are superbly successful. But he was also superb treating less familiar subjects, like *Witchcraft in England* by Christina Hole. When Mervyn illustrated a book, he first soaked himself in the text, until he felt almost a part of it. This was particularly true of Dickens and the drawings he did for *Bleak House*. Each book he read was an education, and Dickens was revelation. The sheer sweep of his creativeness, the vividness of his description, the liveliness of his conversations, the fantastic quality of his imagination and his human oddities: all these struck sympathetic chords in Mervyn's own mind, and had, as he himself insisted, a considerable influence upon what he was already engaged in writing, the 'Gormenghast' trilogy.

I received a letter from Wepham in Sussex, dated 24 October 1943, which is particularly relevant to some of the points I have been discussing.

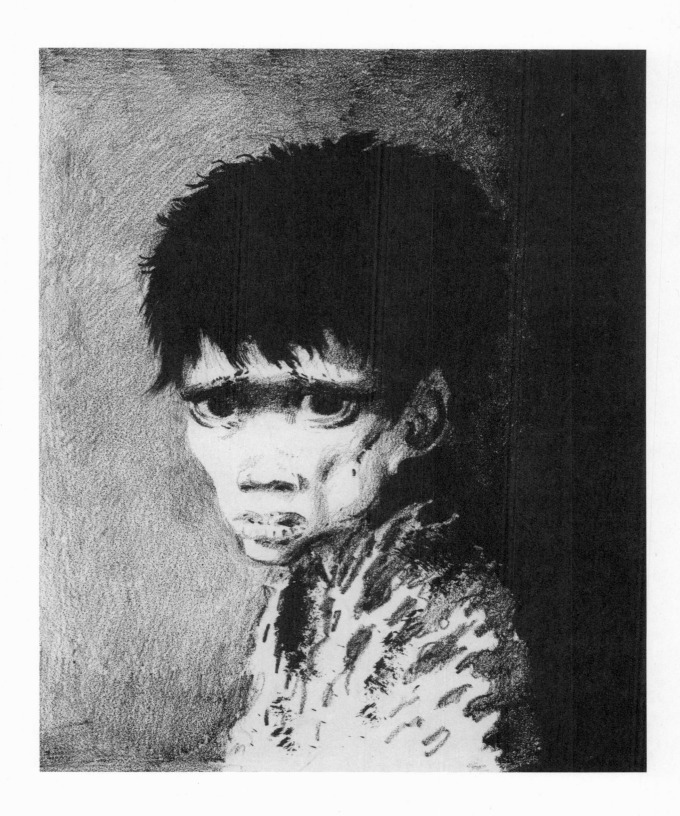

36. *One of the Drawings for* Bleak House—Jo, *the Crossing Keeper (1945)*

Ahoy!

I am writing this in the central white room of our cottage, with old Goodyear, the local wheelwright, smashing a large four-foot-square hole into the flint wall of that dark dungeon-like province to the right as one goes into the kitchen from the house. It has, or rather *he* has let in half the sky and (by the way, it was our idea—he hasn't simply arrived and started making holes in our wall, whim-like!) the late dungeon has become the best-lit room in the house—where meals will be devoured and where I hope you will before the Xmas holidays have come and gone join us in many a heart-stirring conversation, plumbing the depths as it were on a toasting-fork, and sailing into the empyreans of thought on clouds of coffee steam.

One of the pleasantest things that ever happened was our St. Erth—St. Ives day. Definitely a blood-red letter day which sings out, or rather drips through one's mind with the most delicious of gouts.

I have been Grimms-fairy-tale-ing rather concentratedly—as they (Eyre and Spottiswoode) want 70 drawings before Xmas. Not so simple—technically, as I want to get all the costumes, etc., authentic mediaeval, and change my technique from the cross-hatching stuff I've used so far. I think it'll be the best thing I've done so far in illustration. Herewith, by the way, the 'Ancient Mariner', which I hope you'll like—you saw the originals (it now crops up to me) in Chelsea, didn't you? The reduction hurt them somewhat. Incidentally, I saw Ch. and Windus yesterday and they tell me that they unprecedentally got rid of their entire first edition within a week to the retailers but it's under 2000 copies, so perhaps these first ones may be of interest—they hadn't paper enough for a bigger first edition but will have to wait several months.

Presumably the reviews will come out and people trying to buy it won't be able to get it. Just in case any of your friends wanted a copy it would be best to get it right away, either by buying it in a shop or, if not gettable locally, by writing to Ch. and Windus enclosing the price. This sounds a bit swank-acious but it might be worth the tip.

I imagine *An English Library* is impossible to get. I enquired at two or three biggish London shops and they said they sold it out immediately and thought it was hopeless to try to get it. I bought Virginia Woolf's *The Common Reader* and have been enormously impressed. More than anything I've read for a very long time. Have you read it? I expect you have. If not, *do*. It's in two series, and I want to get the second as soon as I can. What it has done is to make me enormously dejected (in the right sort of way, I think) over *Titus Groan*. Her essays on writing and writers—'An Elizabethan Lumber Room', 'The Brontës', 'Montaigne' and many others were so illumined with pure insight and penetration that I felt I could apply all she said—and she has the most catholic taste, surprisingly enough to me—to myself and *Titus* seemed to be suddenly very shabby. In a way I wanted to write to you largely on account of my book for I know you can see exactly what I'm after.

I feel that what I'm 'after' has to a large extent been forgotten while I wrote. What *was* I after anyway? I suppose, to create a world of my own in which those who belong to it and move in it come to life and never step outside into either *this* world of bus-queues, ration-books, or even the upper Ganges—or into *another* imaginative world. I mean that the mood should be always, although I hope varied from chapter to chapter—yet consistently, say, Gryphon, and not Bulldog, Gazelle or even Gargoyle. Always Gryphon (par exemple)—a gryphon that may have a complex temperament and show different coloured scales under different lights—but whose smell must pervade every page—sometimes like Gryphonodour, sometimes Gryphonstench—sometimes Gryphon-of-roses. This I don't think I've done. Maybe I'll have to hack it to hell and re-write whole chapters. It gets too sane in the middle of the book, and the saner it gets—in other words the more it gets like a novel in the library subscribers' sense of the word, the more super-ficial it becomes. At its strangest it is nearest to being spiritual—as against materialistic. Damn novels in the sense of being NOVELS. I want to create between two covers a world, the move-ments of which—in action, atmosphere and speech—enthrall and excite the imagination.

I know this is flying very high but I suddenly feel sick with so much of it. I don't know about the latter part of what you've got—but the first part of my chunk is very like other novels. Nanny Slagg and Fuschia (*sic*) seem intolerably sentimental. Steerpike, wordy, to the verge of tears. Oh God!

There must be some kind of adamantine substance, a foundation of iron, on which things happen—or rather, things must happen and be described with something iron-like, intractable, in the style. I don't mind the periodic splurges of extravaganza, fantasy, etc., but in-between-the-gaps, between the big Incidents, must be crisp—but with the crispness of the Gryphon—that is I think the whole point—the beast that the book *is* must always expose itself.

It is very difficult to understand one's own shortcomings, but do you think this criticism of the bk comes anywhere near the mark? I now feel that *when* it's published doesn't matter— what *does* is that I spare myself no pains in cutting away all the unhealthy and redundant flesh & getting down to a spare, muscular body.

In one way I am very glad that you had not read any of it, for you can read it freshly (poor you!—fresh is probably the last thing you'll be . . . I don't mean you effluviate more than is normal) and I am looking forward to hearing your reactions. Be as ruthless as you feel—the advantages to me will be hard to calculate—for your criticism means the devil of a lot, to me.

Can you send me Dodo's address and army rank? I don't think she can have received my letter thanking her for the match-boxes I asked for, and I'm sure she would have replied. Can you send me Olive's address by the way? She might like to come down to Burpham for a week-end.

Cheerio just for now. We hope, in spite of all your *hideous* characteristics—the most heinous one being your inveterate habit of breathing—that you'll sojourn at the time of the holly and turkey (before, at, or after) beneath our thatch.

Sebastian and Fabian were recovered from the Nursery School and this is their first day at home. Sebastian, a bellyache—I mean he *has* one, and Fabian a niagara nose, such is love and all that's winsome.

Maeve sends her love and best wishes
Yours ever
Mervyn

Below his signature is a pen-drawing of a wimpled hag, hideous even by his standards, with a male of a Byzantine type leering lecherously over her shoulder and playing with what appears to be a Michaelmas daisy. Beside them, he had written: 'His blandishments persisted—but it was no use—she remained adamant, cleaving to her virginity like the born schnozzle she was.'

About a month later he wrote again from Wepham, to thank me for the critical notes I had sent him about the book. The letter begins cheerfully:

Hullo!

Sitting here very smug with a very nice wife on the other side of the fire—true Darby and Joan atmosphere. Howling wind, (*without*, one hopes)—pipe in mouth—trousers on legs—all the bourgeois signs—save three. No goldfish in a bowl on the stove—no aspidistr'y with an 'istory—and NO TEETH. . . .

It ends:

Maeve and I were married six years ago tomorrow—so she sends you a kiss, she says, though the logic rather baffles me. . . .

Mervyn continued to work on *Titus*. For all his hard thinking about the problems involved, there was something compulsive about its 'monstrous birth'. It was, he confessed, as if it were something he had to get out of himself, 'rather like having to be sick'.

Post-War Years

IT IS WORTH emphasizing that when the War ended Mervyn was still only in his early thirties, and at the height of his powers. He painted, and drew, and wrote; he was happily married, and brought up a family; and it seemed as if fame and financial security must at last be on the way. The roll of his publications during the ten years that followed is an impressive tribute to his industry and creativeness, and yet does not include many works—finished or begun—which came out later: for instance, *Titus Alone*, 'A Reverie of Bone', 'The Rhyme of the Flying Bomb', or *The Wit to Woo*. He won the Royal Society of Literature Prize for *Gormenghast* and *The Glassblowers*. His paintings hung on some illustrious walls. . . . It was a time, again, of much hope and great achievement: but full recognition and financial rewards were still very slow to arrive.

After the arbitrary placements of war, the Peakes were back in their old haunts. The cottage at Wepham had proved a happy refuge, and soon they were back in Chelsea. I came to know more of their friends, like Esmond Knight and his wife Nora Swinburne. Whenever we met he was still the same Mervyn: kind, humorous, and full of exciting plans.

I had moved to Taunton School in Somerset, and he came to visit me there; but he was never easy in an institution. Perhaps it was the charming, unpredictable young, moving to their own laws; or perhaps it was being in a closed society, summoned by bells to strange rituals.

37. Illustration from a letter to the Author (Oct 29th 1943)

Sark still attracted him strongly, and he and Maeve decided to go back there to live. I went with them for a short holiday at the Dixcart Hotel, and later stayed with them at their house, Le Châlet, where I became an honorary uncle to Sebastian, my much-neglected godson, and Fabian. Both painted splendid pictures, quite unlike those achieved by their father or mother, and 'Faded' was (many years later) to become a professional artist himself. The two small monsters would come raiding me in pyjamas at an unearthly hour; and later we would go exploring among the still undiscovered cliffs and bays. There was also a pot-bellied donkey of great charm, whose portrait now hangs in a room on Vancouver Island.

Mervyn seemed cheerful. A letter arrived in Somerset towards the end of the Winter Term of 1947, headed 'Sark', but apparently posted in London. The top half of the first page was filled by a drawing: a man, of sorts, sitting on a bench, his face so wide that it actually contained a landscape, with a horse and a sheep, and some decrepit fencing round his right cheek.... Hanging down on his chest was a notice, saying, 'Let this be a WARNING to you!' Various figures, some also nearly human, were flying, or lying, or climbing palm-trees all round the page; and a spectacled creature with a pointed head dangled a large-toothed fish from a slender chain.... Under the broad-faced man was the remark: 'Nature I lov'd and next to Nature—Art. With knobs on.'

The letter itself read:

'How fares the 5 ft. 10 inches of ghastly marl that apes your soul so badly? If you are not scaling some foul peak (don't be so insulting) between the 18th. and the 18th. (Dec. and Jan.), come to the Small Cat House or somewhere else with us. We are staying with Ruth and Matty at their house (18 months in the finding!) at 13 Addison Gardens. It's nearly a year since we've seen you. We want to hear about your work, whether you're happy there. Write here,—Sark. Within two or three days, will you (write)?

Love from us both
Mervyn

Presumably the posting had been delayed.

38. Sarkese (1948)

39. *Sketch for* Dr. Jekyll and
Mr. Hyde *(1948)*

Mervyn and Maeve went to Sark, where their daughter Clare was born; but in the end the encircling seas became perhaps too constricting, and they all returned to Chelsea.

I remember meeting them once in London on their return from the island. It may have been when Sebastian was small: at any rate they arrived at the London terminus with a small child and a mountain of luggage, including a carry-cot and a small enamel jerry. Mervyn and I left Maeve with everything while we went off to find a conveyance. All the taxis seemed to be bespoken, but, to his great delight, Mervyn found what must have been one of the last horse-cabs ever to operate for hire in London. This we engaged, and piled everything inside, to clip-clop off in Edwardian glory. On the way, the baby had to use the pot. Maeve and I tried to distract Mervyn, but in Cambridge Circus he let down the window and, with a grand flourish, emptied the contents of the pot into the street. 'Really!' said Maeve, 'you are *childish*!'

Gormenghast had followed *Titus Groan* into print, and Mervyn was already at work on *Titus Alone*. He wanted, he told me, to include in this volume more of the modern world, its aeroplanes for instance, or pylons, and yet to make them acceptable as part of the ambiance of Gormenghast. I argued, perhaps without completely understanding his intentions, that this might destroy the whole consistent truth or illusion of what he was making; and referred him to his own previous arguments about creating a world in its own right. In the end, he found his own successful compromise or transmutations; and indeed began to consider further developments, to be carried out in a fourth book, which he began.

Mervyn in Sark, 1947

3 Trafalgar Studios
Manresa Rd. Chelsea. SW3.

Dear Soate.

Herewith a most curious request. When
I went to Eyre & Spottiswood ("migraine"
to you) I was appalled at being asked
whether I would condense into about 200
words the "oomph" of Gormenghast.. I
can't think of another word. Sincerity
which will give readers an idea of
what they are letting themselves in
for. The "blurb" in other words.
I said, "Look here", (or some such
opening gambit) "I can't write
my own "blurb" for the dust cover—
its indecent". True, said they
(in effect) but authors have so
scolded us in the past when they
have read the blurbs we've
given them that we are asking
writers to try to say what they've
been driving at — Keeping out
superlative adjectives if they can!

"This is all very well" said I — but
I haven't the faintest idea of
what I've been driving at nor
why the book was ever written. This
shook them somewhat — but they
saw the point vaguely.

Nevertheless they insisted
on my dabbling with my lily-white
fingers in their sewer — & I could
see that they would make a pretty
good hash of the job.

I had a shot or two but
bossed it. All I could write
was. "Candles gutter. Towers of black
ivy drip. Figures move by — loom
& impend: Madness, Tenderness,
lyricism and horror jostle one
another along half-lit corridors in
this, the first volume of a trilogy)

2

40. Part of a letter to the Author,
1947

41. *Maeve* (c. *1950*)

42. *Clowns for Bertram Mills'*
Circus (1948)

He was never a financial genius (though Maeve performed continuing miracles), and now made the mistake of moving to a rather attractive house in the country at Smarden, where on my visits we practised archery on the lawn. But it proved to be far too expensive. Doctor Peake had died in 1950, and left his Sussex cottage, 'Reed Thatch' at Burpham, to Leslie, who had returned, alive but badly shaken, from internment in Changi jail by the Japanese. To Mervyn and Maeve, Doc. left his old house in Wallington. Mervyn wrote, in characteristic vein:

3 Trafalgar Studios,
Manresa Road, Chelsea.
2nd. December 1952.

Goaty, you lop-eared, cross-eyed, gangrenous moron, where the bloody hell have you been hiding your withered body? I suppose you were the last to make an attempt, however—ringing Smarden 255 when we were out.

'He never tried again.'

We've left Smarden and are camping here until we can get to 55 Woodcote Rd. Yes, Wallington, where the Dusky Birron was born. Perhaps he will bloom again and fructify—NO, NO, FRUCTIFY, I said.

Ring (impossible, no phone), write or get in touch somehow and immediately and tell us how many days you can stay with us over your next vacation. We would all love it. If you desert me I'll never forgive you.

Love to all your family when you write. Tons of news when we see you. Love from Maeve and us all—

Mervyn.

The return to Wallington was, as he remarks, a renewal of old ties. Furthermore, when my father retired from the ministry I bought a house for the family only a mile away from Woodcote Road. The purchase was not completed without difficulty, and indeed would never have been completed at all had it not been for a remarkably noble effort by Mervyn! All arrangements had

43. Ben Gunn and Jim Hawkins
*(*Treasure Island*) (1949)*

been made and my offer accepted. Then I received a letter blandly informing me that the owner had taken a better offer. It was a major crisis. Here was I, gazumped, and stranded on the far side of England. All I could think of was to get in touch with Mervyn, who was on the spot, and ask him if he could see the man and persuade him that he was being dishonest.

Mervyn (who had got his telephone back) obviously hated the idea—as who would not?—but he consented to try. To my surprise, and lasting gratification, he succeeded! In the circumstances, I thought his next letter, dated February 1955, was fairly moderate in expression:

Hi!!

Not that you deserve this hand-made elephant-breath notepaper!

Maeve and I are delighted that the transaction has gone through O.K. Thanks for your thanks!

If my passionate, febrile, earthy, sensitive, wart-laden, tear-jerking, phlegmatic, abstract, cock-bitten sentences over the phone helped to tip the scale, then I'm really happy about it. It is a friendly house, with the feel of a home about it—very unlike those other 'kiss of death' ones we saw—built for robots by robots. . . .

The phone he used for this remarkable feat of blackmail and persuasion was presumably his old Wallington number, 9572, which he had first given me over twenty years earlier. 'Nine five seven two?' I had exclaimed. 'How on earth am I to remember a four-figure number like that?' And he had replied, 'By some simple mnemonic, say, er, "Nice fish seldom spew!"' It is a number I still remember.

In spite of financial difficulties (for they still owed a great deal of money on the Smarden property, and the banks—as Mervyn put it in one letter—were becoming 'increasingly militant'), he and Maeve were happy, and still very much in love, in the big old Wallington house. But our proximity there did not last for long. They went back to London, first to Chelsea again, then, when they finally managed to sell the Wallington house, to

Peake '53

44. *Flying Figure (1953)*

1 Drayton Gardens, Kensington, which was to be their home thereafter.

This was a tall, dignified, rather narrow-fronted house, with a basement area and white stone pillars to the portico. It soon became familiar with all the objects and furnishings that had followed them from home to home: his paintings and drawings, the whale's vertebrae, the stuffed pheasants, the row of English poets I had given him for a wedding-present, the set of Proust that only Maeve had read, the two cats, and the huge easel that had been one of his earliest purchases.

There were bedrooms for all the family, and separate rooms where he and Maeve could paint. Few things are more interesting than to stroll about an artist's studio, where canvases are piled on edge against the walls, and to turn one or two of them back in case there is something you haven't seen before, just gathering dust. Artists are careless, even of their best work—and only too generous in disposing of them to their friends!

Mervyn was so prolific and so successful with a pencil or a pen that his work with a brush is sometimes over-shadowed. Was he, then, a painter who did not paint, much, in oils? Those who have been to see his exhibitions in this country or in Dublin will not think so, for his talent was enormous and illumined everything he touched. The Queen Mother owns some of his works; over Lord Olivier's fireplace there hangs (or at any rate used to hang) his portrait of the actor as Richard the Third; and in the possession of his late brother was a bright cockerel as striking as anything by Picasso. Nevertheless, I suppose it is true that he never fully realized his ambitions as a painter in oils—which, rightly or wrongly, is the medium above all in which an artist aspires to shine.

In *The Craft of the Lead Pencil* (a booklet worthy to be set on a shelf beside Housman's *Name and Nature of Poetry*), Mervyn wrote: 'A drawing should be an attempt to hold back from the brink of oblivion some fleeting line or rhythm, some mood, some shape or structure suddenly perceived, imaginary or visual.' Clearly this implies much more than mere reproduction; but his own art was naturally representational and interpretative, and

Maeve in the garden at Wallington, 1952

drawing and writing gave him *immediate* scope. Oils he approached, it may be, with more deliberate self-consciousness, considering 'the picture itself and not what it is about', and composition, and the quality of the paint. This may have been inhibiting, at least in prospect, and one reason why, deeply interested as he was in the techniques and minutiae of oil-painting, he was less often to be found in front of an easel than over a sketch-pad.

An unfinished project of his may be studied in a very large unfinished canvas still in Drayton Gardens. It depicts the apocalyptic vision of a 'little man', from a sordid house, round whom move lovely, spiritual, epicene figures in a kind of dance. . . . It was to have been his *magnum opus* in oils. But it is still at an early stage, the colours have not yet lit, and the sky is dark.

In his life too, the sky was darkening. Mervyn's health began to fail. He was shaken by tremors, and moved more slowly than before.

There were still good days to come, and high hopes and fine occasions. In Drayton Gardens he sat and drew, and smoked his pipe, and wrote; and when we met he was the same Mervyn, and we talked and schemed and went out on sorties; and returned to splendid fry-ups, conjured up at short notice by Maeve, who kept all things together, for all the family.

We planned a new co-operative work to be called *The Artist and I*, though it never really got off the ground, and all I have is four or five pages of sketches and rather jocose dialogue; and he played with the idea of a swarm of drawings, all of things beginning with the same letter, which I was to introduce in verse. These two rather personal examples which I give are of course parerga, but he was still doing valuable work of his own, and *Titus Alone* and 'A Reverie of Bone', to take the two most important examples, had yet to be published.

Then there was the First Night of his play, *The Wit to Woo*, on in the West End, a great and hopeful occasion. Mervyn and Maeve and all their family were there, and my sister Olive and I came too. Shortly before that, he and Maeve even made a trip to Spain, a country and a people that appealed to his sense of the romantic and aloof.

But things grew worse.

Whether the psychological hurts of Mervyn's life: his breakdowns during the War, for instance, or the shock of going to Belsen, would have led to any later impairment of his life, it is now impossible to say. Certainly he had reacted strongly (though

45. *Dog-Man, drawn for* Foot-Fruit, *a book which Peake planned but never wrote* (c. *1955)*

not deliberately) against the discipline and meaningless rituals, as they seemed to him, of life in the forces; and later, in the *Titus* books these become one of his main targets. Of the effects of Belsen it is more difficult to be certain. He did not talk about it very much, except in the most general terms; but to anyone as sensitive to the unhappiness of others and to the value of human dignity and independence as he was, the experience must have been shattering. His poem 'The Consumptive, Belsen 1945' shows this:

> Her agony slides through me: am I glass
> That grief can find no grip
> Save for a moment when the quivering lip
> And the coughing weaker than a broken wing
> That, fluttering, shakes the life from a small bird.

The terrible drawings that go with this poem reproduced in *Drawings of Mervyn Peake* (Grey Walls Press) are also evidence. But the damning portrait of the wardress in Belsen and the grim look into the war criminal in his death-cell (see following pages) show that he was coping with a whole mind. The psychologists and neurologists who saw him seem to have been imprecise in their judgements. It is not always the sensitively vulnerable who lack stamina or come to sudden disaster. He had great powers of recovery, and maintained his creativeness of mind and the integrity of his personality till he was stricken by more purely physical disease. Then, encephalitis and Parkinson's were variously diagnosed. I knew all about Parkinson's Disease. My father had died of it.

At one stage, because there was no appropriate institution available, he was sent to Banstead Hospital. When I visited him he was rather quiet, and certainly shaky, but his conversation was normal and interested, and the male nurses treated him like a friend. It seemed all wrong that he should be there.

Finally, Maeve was told with brutal abruptness by a specialist one day, 'Mrs. Peake, your husband is suffering from premature senility!'

Peake

The Priory, Roehampton

MERVYN BECAME A patient at The Priory, Roehampton, and Maeve managed somehow to support him there. She travelled out to see him on every possible day, and the infrequency of my own visits (though they were necessarily confined to the school holidays) still brings me shame. I would approach from Wimbledon, skirting the Common and turning left near Richmond Park. Opposite the rugger ground, where the Public School Sevens had been played on happier occasions, stood The Priory, like something out of a novel by Mrs. Radcliffe, or a pastiche of Strawberry Hill.

'Can I go up to see Mr. Peake, please?'

This was the only formality needed at the reception desk in the Hall; but I would have to ring a bell for an attendant to unlock the door to the wing in which he lived. This was long, on the first floor, and comfortably equipped with lounges and television; though the sight of so many old men, senile or stricken to slowness by some mental or physical illness, was immediately saddening. Mervyn had a bed-sitter just inside on the left. Often he was not there, but further on, in the lounge, and would appear in the distance, a characteristic but pathetic figure, over on one side for lack of balance, and oddly small and thin, his widow's peak of hair now almost white. As soon as he saw me he would hurry forward as best he could on the attendant's arm, and speak, though it became increasingly difficult to understand what he said.

48. *German Prisoners in a Wood*
   (1945)

49. *The Little Man (1955)*

His room, which was lofty and of a fair size, looked out over lawns and bushes, with a glimpse of Gothic flutings and pointed windows to the left. There was an iron bed with a candlewick coverlet, an empty fireplace, a wardrobe, an armchair, and a table with two upright chairs. A sketch-pad held old sketches, and he read no books. He himself was neatly though shabbily dressed, his coat stained with dribble, but he still wore the bright yellow socks of more colourful days.

Conversation, as I have indicated, was difficult, and therefore embarrassing. In the early days there, at least, he often spoke, eager to communicate and happy to see me; but if I couldn't understand what he had said I had to reply with something vague and unconvincing, or seem to go on with a subject that might be related. He would rise, and go slowly across the room to fetch something, staggering so that I started up to take his arm, and then forget what he wanted and what he had begun to say. In some ways he had, of necessity, grown a little childish, and he took the chocolates I brought with eager but slow and clumsy fingers, while quick strings of saliva came from his lips— reminding me of my father's symptoms. I wiped my wrist furtively against my trousers to dry it, hoping he wouldn't see.

After only too short a time, and increasingly as the months went on, a visit would tend to fizzle out. At first he always came contentedly to the wing door to see me off, and we would wait for the man with the key; later, I made some quick apologetic noise and slipped away, leaving him alone again. Olive, my sister, came once, and kissed him naturally and affectionately; and a couple of times my mother came to wait in the car below, but she could not manage the stairs to his room. Maeve came regularly, bravely cheerful; and her sisters; and his children; otherwise he was increasingly alone.

I think it was at the end of my last visit but one that the friendly white-coated attendant (they all seemed fond of Mervyn) remarked:

'Your father is a little better today, isn't he?' I must have stared, for he asked apologetically, 'He *is* your father, isn't he?'

Mervyn was nearly four years younger than I was.

The next time I came was with Maeve. There was a drawing, a bit stained but rather nice, of a girl, in his sketch-pad, and he offered it to me, dumbly. When I said goodbye, he lifted his face to be kissed, like a good child, a little to our embarrassment. I am not sure he knew quite who I was, but he knew I was friendly.

I never saw him again.